Margaret Veley, Leslie Stephen

A Marriage of Shadows

And Other Poems

Margaret Veley, Leslie Stephen

A Marriage of Shadows
And Other Poems

ISBN/EAN: 9783337005894

Printed in Europe, USA, Canada, Australia, Japan

Cover: Foto ©Thomas Meinert / pixelio.de

More available books at **www.hansebooks.com**

A

MARRIAGE OF SHADOWS

AND OTHER POEMS

BY

MARGARET VELEY

WITH BIOGRAPHICAL PREFACE

BY

LESLIE STEPHEN

PHILADELPHIA

J. B. LIPPINCOTT COMPANY

1889

TO THE FRIENDS OF MY DEAR DAUGHTER,
MARGARET VELEY.

IT is with pleasure and sincere gratitude I have accepted the kind offer of Mr. Leslie Stephen to preface this little volume of Poems. I have done the very best I could for it, and that which I know my daughter would like better than anything else. I must now leave it to go into the world alone, hoping her Friends will appreciate the work of one who is gone.

SOPHIA VELEY.

45 MATHESON ROAD, KENSINGTON, 1888.

PREFACE.

THE life of MARGARET VELEY, author of the following poems, was quiet and uneventful. Her father, Augustus Charles Veley, was the eldest son of a M. de Veley who left Switzerland for England about the beginning of this century. The son became a solicitor in Braintree, Essex, where he was entrusted with much of the ecclesiastical business of the district and was on friendly terms with many of the clergy. On September 3, 1840, he married Sophia, daughter of the Reverend Thomas Ludbey, for over forty years (from 1818 till his death in May 1859) rector of Cranham. Mr. and Mrs. Veley had four daughters, of whom Margaret, the second, was born May 12, 1843. The sisters received an education of the usual kind from governesses and masters ; and Margaret passed one term at Queen's College, Tufnell Park. She became a good French scholar. She and her elder sister competed for prizes in composition offered by a

French educational journal.   Although she won no prizes, she often obtained honourable mention.   She became so familiar with the language that her companions on a foreign tour found it impossible to puzzle her by asking her for the names of out-of-the-way objects.   She rarely ventured to talk French, but she was fond of the litera- ture and very familiar with many of the best modern writers, poets, novelists, and critics.   She began to write English verse at an early age.   Some specimens are preserved among her papers.   A little religious poem is dated just before her fourteenth birthday ; and others of a similar character follow.   At a rather later date she ventures upon a mock-heroic legend of the 'Blue Princess,' suggested by the contagious qualities of the dye of a friend's dress.   The Princess has begged the gift of learning from a fairy godmother, who has an old- fashioned antipathy to 'blue' ladies ; and spitefully im- parts the gift not only in an allegorical but in a literal sense, with ingenious and disastrous consequences. Miss Veley says in one of her letters that to publish a book had been among her day-dreams even in her nursery.   She taught in a Sunday-school and had great power of attracting the affections of her pupils.   Some of them continued to write to her about their plans and prospects long after they had left the place.   She gave up teaching upon the advent of a new clergyman, whose views differed so much from her own that cordial co-operation became impossible. Miss Veley had reached conclusions very different from those which naturally found favour with the home circle. She was a very decided liberal both in political and religious matters. Her singularly modest and retiring character prevented her from ever putting forward her views in an aggressive fashion. She remained upon the most affectionate terms with persons from whose views she entirely dissented. Her divergence from the conservative and high-church principles of her closest connections showed the real independence of thought which was generally concealed by her extreme gentleness of manner.

Her first published poem, called 'Michaelmas Daisies,' appeared in the 'Spectator' of April 1870. In the September of the same year a short story called 'Milly's First Love' appeared in 'Blackwood's Magazine,' which has so often given the first welcome to literary talent. A considerable interval, however, elapsed before the next publication. She always wrote slowly and with most conscientious workmanship. Part of the time was occupied in the composition of 'For Percival' (begun in March 1872) and of most of the poems collected in this volume. I gather, too, that she had to undergo a disappointment about a short story which failed to win immediate favour from an editor. Her extreme diffidence

made her sensitive in such matters. She believed, as
she said, in failure more easily than success ; though she
was not so much discouraged by criticism as incited to
take more pains to avoid the alleged defects. Her poem
the 'Japanese Fan' appeared in the 'Cornhill Magazine'
for September 1876. I was then editor, and she sent
me the poem with a letter of introduction from her
friend, Mr. Meredith Townshend, for whose services in
the way of literary advice and encouragement she often
expressed her gratitude. This was followed by 'Lizzie's
Bargain,' which appeared in the 'Cornhill' of May and
June 1877 ; and by her longer story 'For Percival,' which
appeared in the same magazine September 1877 to
December 1878. This novel appeared (and still appears)
to me to be marked by very rare qualities which are not
always to be found in more popular novels. It had true
literary distinction : a graceful, clear, and pointed style,
a strong sense of humour, and a keen perception of
character approached by few of her contemporaries. It
excited much interest, and I fancy would have been
still more successful if it had possessed some more
commonplace attractions. The end was painful, whereas
most readers—and I do not say that they are wrong—
like things to be made pleasant. A dismissal of the
characters to general happiness would have been out of
harmony with the melancholy tone of the whole story.

The book, however, was warmly welcomed by many readers and brought to her some valuable friendships. Mr. Luke Ionides introduced himself by an appreciative letter to the unknown author; and she ever afterwards reckoned Mr. and Mrs. Ionides among her most attached friends.

Many domestic troubles saddened some years of her life. The sister next to her in age, Mrs. Holmes, was sent to Penzance in 1876 for her health, and Miss Veley nursed her through an illness which terminated fatally in July 1877. Their father died on January 19, 1879. The other sisters were married, and Miss Veley, with her mother, decided to leave Braintree for London, where she made her home for the rest of her life. The delicacy of her youngest sister, Constance, who in 1878 had married Mr. Alfred E. Warner, enforced journeys in search of health. Mrs. and Miss Veley accompanied her to Switzerland and the Riviera ; but she became decidedly worse in 1884, and afterwards remained in London, where she was nursed by her sister until her death in May 1885.

The shadow of these sorrows may be traced in Miss Veley's later writings. 'Mrs. Austin appeared in the 'Cornhill' of April and May 1880; 'Damocles' in the 'Cornhill' of February to December 1882 ; 'Mitchelhurst Place' in 'Macmillan's Magazine' of 1884; 'A Garden of Memories' in the 'English Illustrated Magazine' of July, August,

and September 1886 ; and 'Twice by the Sea' in the
'Hourglass' of July 1887.

During her life in London, Miss Veley became known
to a much larger circle capable of sympathising with her
literary tastes than could be found in the country town
where she had passed the first thirty-five years of her life.
She was not quite in her element in general society.
She was constitutionally shy, even to a painful degree,
and the shyness was probably intensified by extreme
shortsightedness.   She began, too, with a large share
of that awe for literary luminaries, even when not of the
first order of magnitude, which is natural before one has
been admitted behind the scenes.   New acquaintance
had to begin by a process of breaking the ice, which
might possibly form again before another interview.   But
with a few thoroughly sympathetic friends, this obstacle
disappeared from the first ; and, to all who met her, the
shyness was felt as an appeal for considerate treatment
and gave to intercourse with her the charm of the
gradual and timid revelation of a strong intellectual and
moral nature.   In my own relations to her as editor of
some of her writings, I was afraid to offer advice, not lest
it should be rejected, but lest it should be too respect-
fully entertained.   The only advice which I could really
offer—perhaps it is all the advice that can be judiciously
offered to any one—was that she should be herself.   And,

indeed, though she was singularly amenable to criticism and perhaps too easily depressed, she did not yield until her judgment was convinced; and her aims were too clearly defined to be easily diverted in essential matters. I must add that she received well-meant suggestions with more than good nature, with a gratitude which was only too full a repayment of the intended service. She had too much magnanimity and was too completely free from vanity to be touchy, although she might be sensitive under criticism ; and, as one of her feminine friends re- marks to me, had the strong sense of justice in which her sex is generally said to be deficient. She was incapable of any petty resentment or of an exaggerated estimate of her own claims.

I must mention one minor virtue in which she was pre-eminent. I have seen many handwritings in the course of my experience as an editor; but never one equal to hers. It was firm, large, and as legible as print, and yet full of character and delicacy. She used to send verses to her friends upon their birthdays or similar occasions, written upon Christmas cards in this exquisite hand which made them real works of art. I give one or two specimens of these little poems, which will prove, I think, that the charm was not confined to the calligraphy.

Miss Veley was gaining a stronger hold upon the affections of all her acquaintance ; and even her less intimate friends were hoping that the reserve which still remained was gradually thawing. The last occasion cn which I had the pleasure of seeing her was in the summer of 1887, and I was then struck by the animation and point with which she discussed some literary topics with a young American admirer of her books. After recovering from the depression produced by the long attendance upon her sister's death-bed she had again settled to literary work, and was writing a novel, which, as she promised her friends, was to have a cheerful catastrophe. She had shown symptoms of delicacy and had never been robust. No alarm, however, had suggested itself to her friends, who were shocked by the news of her death on December 7, 1887, after a very short illness, caused by a chill and ending in an affection of the throat. She was buried on December 10, in Braintree Cemetery by the side of her father and her sister Alice. Her mother and her elder sister, Mrs. Webb, survive.

The unfinished novel just mentioned was to be another sketch of the country life which she knew so well. She had made a careful outline of the whole story with dates and genealogical relations clearly plotted out. She had finished the first volume, and the fragment shows, I think, that her powers were still ripening, although it is too incomplete and too much in the nature of an introduction to justify publication. Her thorough workmanship made rapid execution impossible ; and her perfect handwriting suggests that she never hurried even in her letters. She could not be slovenly. She was never satisfied until she had gained all possible clearness of definition in her thought as in her manual work. She was in this respect in sympathy with the French writers whose congenial qualities she appreciated so keenly. In English, she especially admired George Eliot, Thackeray, and Miss Austen, the last of whom she preferred to Scott. An old friend, Mr. Lewis Day, has shown me a curious little controversy which they conducted upon post-cards as to the rival claims of ' realism ' and ' idealism.' It was an excellent plan apparently for securing a condensed statement of the points at issue ; but condensation generally involves a little obscurity. A phrase or two will indicate her view sufficiently. ' I do think,' she says, ' that a man should aim at simply reproducing the facts of nature, as he sees them, in his work. Men see things so differently that the most literal transcript is sure to be a revelation to his fellow men. The more literal the transcript, the greater the revelation.' Realism has, she thinks, the charm ' of representing the *apparently* hap-hazard complexity of life which seems to have forced itself upon the modern mind. Some of us would rather have even broken and confused reflections of the great real world, than the prettiest little worlds the idealists can arrange

a

for us.' ' If the order and repose ' (of the idealist) ' are
more than are truly consistent with the weakness and
inevitable miseries of human life, it seems to me very
like consoling oneself for the earthiness of the globe by
blowing pretty soap bubbles. . . . I want what gives me a
sense of reality.' To the objection that realism means
commonplace, she replies: ' I see no redemption from
commonplace, except by the teaching that the springs of
tears and laughter and deepest tenderness break forth in
the very midst of the vast commonplaces of life.'

Her novels were realistic in this sense, which
might have been adopted by her beloved Miss Austen.
They were meant to give an accurate portraiture of life
as she saw it. But her novels were not merely photo-
graphic reproductions of the first scenes that came to
hand. They are always embodiments of some genuine
idea. After discussing one of her stories she adds :
' And then came the inevitable problem, without which
I have hitherto been unable to get on. Was such a
renunciation as Lizzie's right? I don't solve my pro-
blems, unluckily--at least I only partially solve them.'
The reason, perhaps, generally seems to be that in this
' haphazard ' world the only solution which she can see
involves the self-sacrifice of some generous nature to the
happiness of more commonplace people. The sadness
which she had to experience is reflected in her fiction

where some unlucky combination of circumstances is generally too much for noble aspirations. But her view of life, if mournful, is anything but cynical. Her world has got into awkward complications ; but she takes the view of the kindly humorist who admits that there is something perverse about the fates, but seeks for consolation not in a blind sentimentalism but in dwelling upon the fine qualities brought out by misery and discord.

Miss Veley had carefully revised her poems, and discussed them with very intelligent self-criticism. Although some of them show the same qualities as her prose, they also reveal a very different side of her nature. She observes, in reference to the obvious remark that there is 'too much sadness' in her poetry: 'I should write more of the brighter poems, perhaps, if I did not write any prose. It is not that I think the brighter thoughts less fit for poetry, but rather that I think the sadder ones less fit for prose. All my feelings of awe and doubt and wonder, and all my longings to get down to the heart of things seem to me to find far deeper and truer expression in verse. Is it that they want to be set to music in some way ? Besides, I can say in verse what I could not say in prose.' Another passage may serve as a comment on some poems, and as a proof of the careful thinking-out of her expression. Her

correspondent had proposed to alter the following passage in 'A Shadow on the Dial :'

> I gain a glimpse of something more than joy
> Higher than rapture, distant as a star,
> A time beyond all time, a steadfast gaze
> And *an abiding thought*, when my weak heart,
> Lifted above self-consciousness, shall beat
> In unison with His.

It was proposed to substitute 'a thought that still
abides.' She explains : ' In my idea, the thought has
no connection with the act of hoping here ; it *is* what I
hope for hereafter. The steadfast gaze and abiding
thought make—as far as I can at present see—my dim
idea of the goal I hope to reach. One gets glimpses now
of beauty and perfection—of God—but one can't look
long—the poorest and meanest things have power to dis-
tract one, even apart from imperfection and dimness of
vision. So I long for "a steadfast gaze." And, though
there is no such happiness here as the feeling of light
dawning on one's mind, new ideas flowing in, new certainty that all is good, it needs an effort. One can
climb a mountain on whose summit one could not live ;
one reads slight and worthless things for rest ; but I
look for a time when I shall not be weary and dull, nor
incapable of grasping the ideas I need, nor painfully
limited. Only fancy—an abiding thought, an ever-widen-

ing universe round one ! ' She then alters the phrase to
' an ever-widening thought.' Speaking of another phrase
in the same poem,

There is no death—life only ; death is nought,

she says : 'Again, I meant the words *literally*, as "an
abstract assertion." Doubts of immortality, ordinary ideas
as to what may follow our dying—absence of definite
knowledge as to what may follow on the other side of
the grave—make Death terrible. But I was fancying that
to this man, when he opened his eyes, the incident of
being transferred from one stage of existence to another
would fall into its place, merely as an incident in his *life.*'
I will not add any remarks of my own, which would,
I think, be impertinent to any sympathetic reader.

A good many letters have been 'sent to me by Miss
Veley's friends, and they show abundantly the tenderness,
the sympathy with sorrow, and the warm gratitude for
all friendly recognition, which gave her a peculiar place
in their affections. Her death seems to have affected
all who knew her with a special sense of loss. I do not
think, however, that any long quotations would be
desirable in this brief notice ; and I will only add a
passage or two to illustrate the rather grave and gentle
humour, which was very characteristic and came out
especially in her playful relations with children. This,
for example, is a history of certain cats in whom a young

friend of hers was interested :—' L. and I,' she says, 'have been weighing them. That is to say, L. went down in the dead of night among the beetles, and single-handed he grappled with Zo(roaster), and weighed him : 2 lbs. 9 oz. Then he wanted me to go down with him and weigh Cy(rus). I went. We got out all the weights in the house, and a flat iron ; but we needn't have bothered about that : he *just* didn't weigh *all* the weights—i.e. he was about 7 lbs. 15 ozs. when we added them all up. Then we metaphorically turned up our sleeves, looked at each other, and went for Thomas Claudius. He weighed :—

   1 violent scrimmage,
   1 scratch (*I* had that).
   1 scale kicked out of its place, and clattering in
      the silence of the night.
   1 tempestuous departure through the doorway.

I haven't added these up ; so I can't exactly tell what they amount to.

'I wish Cy and T. C. D. wouldn't think my sunflowers ought to be sat on like eggs . . . As for Zo he is simply and literally " the Desolator," as Byron has it . . . When I was planting out seedling asters the other evening, in a hurry, because the light was failing, he said quite distinctly, " A Zoro-aster is better than a China-aster any

day," and proceeded to plant himself in every hole in
turn. Being with difficulty uprooted, he climbed and
bounced about till the next hole was ready.'

In another note she gives an analysis of the same
garden. 'There are in 100 parts :

Stones (say) 76
Potsherds, brickbats, bones, bits of glass, and
    a rusty iron bar which L. dug up (say) . 14
Worms, grubs, &c. 7
Bits of newspaper, and varied rubbish always
    mysteriously arriving. Think they grow,
    but about 2

And there you are. I don't go in for infinitesimal traces
of things. I'm only a beginner, you see ; but I call this
a good bold analysis in round numbers. If you add it up
you'll find it comes to just 100—no, it doesn't, it comes
to 99. What little trifle have I forgotten? Well, it can't
much matter, can it? . . . O, but I have it :

Earth 1

That's it. Now it's all right.'

And this is a little specimen of an Alpine adventure.
Her companion's aunt wanted a particular kind of
gentian. 'We could have accommodated her with a cart-
load of almost anything else, but *that* we could not find,
and everything was dripping wet, everywhere. I have

seldom seen anything more pathetic than A. standing
in the middle of a flowery, grassy, boggy, Alpine slope,
very anxious to get back to dry ground, but restrained by
a noble sense of duty to his aunts and conscientiously
examining every bluebell or harebell, of which there were
at least 50,000 round him.   Harebells here do grow
abominably blue when you are looking for gentians.   I—
with the water running into my boots—admired him.
We never got our gentian after all ! He found one,
which I would not let him dig up, because it wasn't the
right sort ; afterwards it turned out that it was a much
rarer one and ought to have been secured at any cost !
Then we encountered a Swiss wayfarer of ferocious
aspect, whose clothing was mainly constructed of holes,
with just stuff enough to keep them apart, and whose
portable property consisted solely of a large knife.   As
he amiably wished us good morning, we hoped that he
was really pleasanter than he looked, and perhaps only
intended to cut wood—in which case of course he
couldn't help his knife, and it wasn't fair to judge him
by it.   At that rate, I suppose, in a lonely woodland spot,
one might misunderstand Mr. Gladstone ! '

   Her letters are full of such humorous descriptions of
little adventures, mixed with remarks upon the scenery,
and upon cathedrals and pictures, in which she took a keen
and intelligent interest.   I will only venture to add a

quotation bearing upon one of her poems, the 'Level Land.' She was uncomfortable at having used the poetically commonplace flowers, amaranth and asphodel, and looked them out in a French dictionary. 'And they said that amaranth was " Love lies bleeding !" " Prince's feather " &c. Milton's angels crowned with that ! . . . I attacked a book in thirty-six volumes on English botany and hunted up a wild amaranth. And Milton's amaranth grows " hard by the tree of life," if I remember right. The description of my wild amaranth began : " This dunghill plant grows chiefly in the neighbourhood of London ' ! ! Coming down in the world, amaranth appears to have acquired low tastes.' She is reminded of ' Moly ' of which she used to read in Pope's ' Odyssey,' and looks it up ' for old acquaintance sake. Horror ! These four authorities, all I consulted, were unanimous. It is a wild garlic, with yellow flowers ! After that . . . I can but hope the Lotos-eaters lay very still ; for the only wild garlic I know, *if crushed* . . . Asphodel is better, though it was a shock to me to learn that it has a nutritive and medicinal root, shaped like a small turnip ! I don't know what that signifies, and they call it " King's spear," which I don't dislike. Strictly speaking, the correct asphodel is rather a stiff spear, with smallish flowers, golden yellow, a little something of brownish gold in it, at intervals up it. . . . I came to the conclusion that I know no more of amaranths

*b

and asphodel than I did before, since the poets' flowers—
Mr. Tennyson's for instance—are evidently not related to
their earthly namesakes.'

In all her letters I have not seen a single phrase of
unkind or even sarcastic tendency, although she has to
mention some experiences which might have justified irri-
tation. They show a most tender and affectionate nature,
bearing grief and disappointment bravely and tenderly,
welcoming all kindnesses with warm goodwill, and light-
ing up little annoyances with a play of gentle humour.

I must offer my thanks to Miss Veley's intimate
friends, especially Mrs. Luke Ionides, Mrs. Macquoid,
and Mr. Lewis Day, who have given me every informa-
tion in their power. Mrs. Veley has entrusted me with
the duty of editing these poems, as a last memorial of
the remarkable talent of the daughter who was never
separated from her through life.

I have also to thank the proprietors of the 'Century,' 'Harper's Magazine,' 'Macmillan's Magazine,' the
'Spectator,' and the 'Bairns' Annual' for permission to
publish the poems which first appeared in their pages.

CONTENTS.

———◆◇◆———

A MARRIAGE OF SHADOWS.

ROUND the flickering fire of life, in the dusky border-
land,
Between the gloom and the glow, the wavering shadows
stand.

Silent for evermore they lie in wait for our eyes,
And he who has looked on them once shall see them
until he dies.

The runner carries his torch, he is glad at heart to see
The triumph of golden light, whence the parting shadows
flee.   ·

He runs with his face aglow, the flame flies out on the
wind,
And the scoffing shadow shapes exult as they leap behind.

B

Short is the life of man ere he draws the evil lot,
Then must he die with the day, and the morrow behold
    him not.

To the silent Valley he comes, where, drifted under the
    steeps,
Are the sands of lives run out, in dead, forgotten heaps.

There is none at hand to help ; the desert earth of his
    bed
Is marked with the treading of feet, but they that have
    trodden are dead.

He lies with his face to the East, while out of the
    vanished years
Come the shadows of bygone days, the shadows of hopes
    and fears.

The shadows of things unknown, that stir in the gulf of
    the night,
That float on the waveless tide, and sink ere the morning
    light.

The shadows of passing thoughts, the shadows of ill
    deeds done,
That stand for a terrible sign between his soul and the sun.

And last, in their glory and grace, in a haze of splendour
    seen,
Come the shadows, saddest of all, from the Land of
    Might Have Been.

They fade in the far off sky, they never shall come
    again,
And the beauty of hopeless dreams is bitterer far than
    pain.

'I have done with shadows,' he cries, 'let them pass
    from my weary heart,
In the West is the face of Death, I will see his face and
    depart.'

What man has seen his face? Over the drifts of the
    sand
Lengthens the Shadow of Death, uplifting a shadowy
    hand.

I.

SUNSET.

An arch of cloudless sky
Rises above a town of ancient name ;
Across its dome
The birds fly home,
And all the West is burning with slow flame,
For night is nigh.
Against the sunset fires,
In broken ranks,
Gables and slender spires
Stand black and crowded on the river's banks ;
And a great bridge is lifted up on high
Above the rippling tide,
Where laden vessels spread their wings and sail
O'er waters wide.
Out of the Eastern region, pure and pale,
The silver flood
Comes, murmuring softly of a thousand rills
From shadowy hills,
But, like a chronicle of conquering pride,
Ends in imperial splendour red as blood.

High stands the bridge, while far below
The river, winding round the weedy piles,
  Whispers, embracing them.   Its onward flow
  Breaks in unchanging curves, like carven smiles,
And strains with snake-like force, and seeks their
    overthrow.

    Across the sunlit height
    Pass and repass the throng
Of men who go their way—the western light
Bright on their living faces—side by side
    With shadows grey and long.
With slim fantastic shapes that slip and glide,
    Follow and run,
That lurk, and waver in uncertain flight
    And fear the sun.

    But one man stands apart,
And facing all the glory of the skies,
Broods o'er an evil world that lies
    Within his heart.
Shadows and men alike before him pass
As nought, as dim reflections in a glass,
As idle shifting figures in a dream.
Unheeded, as the sunlit ripples roll,

They come and go,
A living stream,
In long procession linked against the glow.
Empty and vain to him the boundless heavens seem,
Vain all the glory of the golden rays,
While with an inward gaze
Darkly intent he shapes a narrow scheme.

But lightly on his face
Does one fair shadow fall,
Lingers a moment on his mouth, close-lipped—
Glides all unheeded to his breast
As if she sought his heart for resting-place
And end of all—
Then, as from mouth to heart she slipped,
Falls downward, mute and sweet
Even to his feet,
Touching the darkness of his shadow, pressed
Against the wall.

Thus do the shadows meet,
Yet she who passes him is worlds away
In her pure loveliness.
As though she were the queen of some pale star,
Alone, afar,

Set high for worship if too high to bless,
Golden amid the dusk of dying day.

As she goes by the hearts of men awake,
Leaving their selfish joy and selfish grief
          For her fair sake,
Rising at sight of her to nobler thought,
          Even as the sap
Flows at the touch of spring to flower and leaf—
         But this one man sees nought.

Yet—does he move in sullen weariness ?
         Or pricked by venomed sting
Of some remembered folly or mishap ?
Or in the windings of his sorry plot,
Perceive the goal, and stand prepared to spring ?
         This I know not,
         But none the less
When glides from him that slender shade of hers
         His shadow stirs.

II.

THE LAND OF SHADOWS.

Night comes and lays her hand
Upon the brows and eyes of toiling men—
Why should they longer seek to understand?
She folds the world in darkness—wherefore keep
A weary flame, a point of wakeful pain,
To fret her dewy stillness cool and deep?
    They yield their souls to sleep,
       Nor know that then
Through universal dusk of hill and plain
Their shadows fly afar to Shadowland.

Dim is that unknown road and ashen-grey
    And no man travels it,
Only from time to time a restless crowd
    Of shadows flit
    Along the level way,
Mocking, as one might mock who laughed aloud,
Though Death itself is not more mute than they.

    Strange is that road, and desolate,
      Narrow as Fate,

On either hand lie glimmering plains of cloud
    Fading afar to night ;
Above, a starless heaven is bowed,
      Whose desert height
    Is pale with unknown light.

Strange is the pathway—strange the final shore—
    A hollow earthen-coloured waste
    (That might be a forgotten world
    From life and splendour hurled),
Girt by a mountain range, lies low for evermore,
      Shrunken and dead.
    The zone of barren rock,
Fantastic, writhen, tortured as with fire,
Cloven by unimaginable shock,
    Shoots up in pinnacle and spire
Against the pallid stillness overhead.
      Within its stony maze
    Are narrow valleys, and steep ways,
      And gulfs that sink
    Sheer from their crumbling brink,
And clefts that hold a darkness so intense,
      One needs must think
It more than night itself, and look to see
Some blackest vision, stirring heavily
      Uprise and issue thence.

Below the frowning heights
Barren, far-reaching, lies the level plain,
Alive with phantoms that in circles vain
Dance through the silence of the windless nights,
 Even as in autumn-tide
The withered leaves, down drifted to the dust,
  Dance to an eddying gust.
 They wheel and mingle and divide
  While far on high
Wild meteors flame across the glimmering sky
To perish when their hasty race is run.
In swift pursuit the shadows leap and fly
 Maddened with liberty,
Mocking the memory of the noonday sun
That held them crouching 'neath his steadfast eye.

They dance for ever as they danced that night,
 When the red sunset light
Had faded from the hills, the shore, the stream,
From the wide sky, and from the eyes of men.
 And, mixing in their flight
 The queenly shadow passed
That on the bridge at eventide was cast,
  Fair now as then.
The light itself could scarcely sweeter seem,

And swift cloud-shadows could no softlier fall,
Than she who fled with every flying gleam,
    Not looking back
Where, on the heedless windings of her track,
    Unmarked by all,
    Came fierce and fast
The shadow that had lurked beneath the wall.

    But, ere he reached her side,
The crowding shapes that wavered to and fro
      Parted to show
    A band of figures placed
Alone amid the wide and level waste.
    Calmly did they abide,
      Like those who wait
    The certain stroke of fate,
And the quick coming of an unknown thing.
These were the shadows of those hapless ones
Who saw that day their last of setting suns,
    To whom, at eventide
    Flew Death on low swift wing ;
    And as on earth they died,
Their shadows felt the pitiless command,
    Drooped 'neath the unseen spell,
    And died in Shadowland.

Closely the swarming phantoms pressed,
And ever nearer drew
Unto those few,
A shifting silent ring,
As if the twilight, gathering darkly round,
Quickened to shapes of tremulous unrest.
Silent they were,
Silent the waiting band,
Only with waving hand
They bade farewell,
But in clear regions of the upper air,
Unto the utmost bound
And limit of the mountain wilderness,
Sang mournful Echo, shadow of a sound,
Alone and bodiless,
Echo of sadness, echo of despair.

' O ye who die this night,
Your race is run,
Of changeful dusk and light
Your thread was spun,
And now your doom is written—you must go.

' Behold, Death comes to break
All woven bands.
What though sad hearts shall ache ?

Loose, loose your hands,
No loving clasp can hold you—you must go.

'There is no man can save—
Your life is past—
The dim mysterious wave
Is rising fast,
The unknown Shadow waits you—you must go.

'Has that wide sea a shore?
No man can know—
In darkness evermore
We hear it flow,
And the great deep has called you—you must go.

'Cry not with dying breath,
All pleading fails—
The bitter wind of death
Has filled your sails—
Farewell—farewell—farewell! for you must go.'

At the last note the shapes distinct and clear,
Sable upon the silver atmosphere,
Grew strange, like phantoms in a mystic glass;
And knowing death was near,
Flung high their arms, as who should moan Alas!

For gladness that had been,
Had been, but should not be—
Then died into the tender dusk unseen,
And with the last a terror seemed to pass,
And all the watching shadows were set free.

Then the pursuer, starting from his place,
Turned swiftly to the chase,
Pressing so closely on the shadow maid
That, conscious of besetting force,
Of strength that followed and that could not tire,
She faltered, half-afraid
And, pausing in her course,
Against her will, she turned, and looked him in
the face.

Dusk shape of Love, with neither flesh nor fire,
Intent, impalpable and mute,
A subtle, haunting phantom of desire,
A shadow of pursuit,
To conquer or beguile
Aping in spectral form his master's way of wile—
He followed her—and she
O with how sweet a grace,
As of an angel stooping from above,
She looked upon him !   Unto what pure love

Had her fair lady, in a dream may be,
Thrilling, half-yielded, tenderly afraid ?

But even as she swayed,
As one who yields, and yet who fain,
Would flee and yield in vain—
High, where the jagg'd horizon cut the air,
There burst a wild and widening glare
Of unknown day upon those twain.
Rushing from dawn to night
A strange white sun
Flashed in a sudden splendour to the height,
And in its light
The flying shadow shapes were fused in one.

III.

ON THE BRIDGE.

Day came again—
  The host of Shadowland
Started in terror from their dusky mirth,
And looking backward as they fled to earth,
    Saw the long bridge of ashen cloud that spanned
      The glimmering plain,
Dissolving swiftly in the sunlit air.
The brooding vapours, heavy as despair,
    Rolled from the lucid sky ;
The winds amid the leafy woodlands stirred,
    And hastening by
Bore happy life, and freshness of the dew,
Odours of plants, and song of careless bird,
      To bid men hope anew,
Buds burst in flower, and waters everywhere
Rippled with joy of morning, frank and fair.

  The slender shadow shape
Fled homeward, seeking to escape
    The light of day ;

Homeward by hedges white with may
  She made her way
  Airy and fleet
  Unto her lady's feet,   .
And found her resting still in slumber sweet.
  There patiently she lay
Until her mistress, gazing with clear eyes,
Looked forth in glad surprise,
  As if the earth, the sky, the flowers,
Were strangely fair to her awakened sight,   .
Though yet she mused upon the midnight hours
Which bore her, drifted on their drowsy streams,
    Through regions of delight,
    Where whitest dreams
Blossomed in all the dusky fields of night.

Meantime the bridegroom shadow in his place,
  Crouched by his master's side, malign and dumb,
  Waiting until the waking hour should come,
    The hour that strips
The veil of darkness from Life's withered face—
  Too soon it came,
    He woke with eyes reluctant, and his lips
  Were bitter with the dregs of half-remembered
    shame.

C

The summer day went by.   The great sun burned
   Upward to kingly noon ;
And through the day the wheeling shadows turned ;
    Till, when their lord sank down,
   Thin vapours drifted o'er the crescent moon.
River, and shore, and hill
   Lay black and small beneath the solemn height,
The grassy fields, the lonely ways were still,
Save for sweet singing of the night-bird brown,
But through the darkened mazes of the town
   Ran busy lines of light.

   Bridegroom and bride
   From the far land of dreams
Banished at golden daybreak, met once more,
    When daylight died,
   Where the great bridge from shore to shore
Glittered across the darkness of the night.
    The lamps set high
    Against the windy sky,
   Cast dim, half-sunken gleams
Upon the dusky rushing of the tide,
   And evermore the hurrying crowds went by.
    The man among them passed
    Not now on sombre thought intent,
But with an aspect of defiant pride,

And glancing as he went,
Saw how a shadow lengthened out to meet
His shadow where it swaggered at his side,
Till twain were one beneath the passer's feet.
Then lifting careless eyes,
He felt within his soul a strange remembrance rise.

Was she a shadow who that shadow cast?
A shadow out of long-forgotten days
Falling across the life she once made bright?
Well might he stand and gaze—
Had the dull years turned backward in their flight
To give him once again
Rapture keen-edged with pain,
The living vision of a dead delight?
Was this his love, the lodestar of his youth?
It could not be! His love lay low,
Never again her weary head to raise—
Sad eyes were closed in sleep,
No more to weep,
Sad lips were sealed, and should no more complain,
Sad heart was still, no sorrow more to know—
And yet she seemed his love in very truth!
So young, so fair, perforce he held his breath,
As if new life had blossomed out of death,
To bring him back that love of long ago.

Within his soul the Past arose once more—
The hour they parted, and the song she sung,
The eyes that followed, and the hands that clung.
Once more he stood where oft he stood before ;
The yellow sun was sinking in the west,
The tide, far off, was ebbing on the shore,
  The orchard boughs
Were white with blossom, for the year was young.
Once more he saw, once more he saw and heard,
  Once more he felt her pressed
Closely against his side ;
  Strong in his whispered vows,
  Scorning all fear of change
Singing her song of sun and leaf and tide,
  Till, at a farewell word,
  Her voice from its high range
Dropped in sharp anguish, like a wounded bird—
Dropped suddenly, and died
In spent and quivering sobs upon his breast.

  Ah, who should sing the rest ?
Forgotten many a year those notes had been,
  But now they woke again,
  Pale Memory took up the broken strain,
And sang it through, with all the sobs between.

'Go, Love, go—if needs it must be so—
  Go, as the Sun goes down his western way
    At dying of the day,
    And all the earth is wrapped
    In shadows chill and grey.

'Go, Love, go—if needs it must be so—
  Go from my longing as the Summer goes ˙
    From many a garden close,
    And through the branches bare
    The wind of autumn blows.

'Go, Love, go—if needs it must be so—
  Go as the Tide, that, sobbing, makes its moan
    O'er sand and weedy stone,
    And yet is drawn perforce
    Unto the deep unknown.

'Go, Love, go—if needs it must be so—
  Summer, and Sun, and Surges of the main,
  Ye cannot heed my pain !
Go, Love, go—if needs it must be so ;
But come, Love, come !—O Love, come thus again !
Come as they come, Love, going as they go !'

  The momentary dream
Was past, the wedded shadows torn apart,

The man once more alone, yet in his heart
   The song was clear and loud,
   Above the Babel of the crowd,
Above the ceaseless ripple of the stream,
   And as he hastened on his way he stepped
      To snatches of its music, sad as tears.
      The haunting voice sang ever in his ears,
   ' Come thus again ! O Love, come thus again ! '
   Mixing it with the notes of ' vain ' and ' pain,'
      And that refrain
      At which of old she wept
Came back to him now all the tears were shed
.Out of the regions of the dead,
      An empty echo, ringing through the years.

He had not listened while she lived to pray
' Come thus again—O Love, come thus again ! '
But now that all the prayer was meaningless,
Now that he could not comfort her one day,
   Nor with his presence bless,
   Nor wipe away
The weary tears which were as fallen rain—
He turned as one who might no more delay,
As if she bade him follow to some place
Without the city, where in loneliness
   He should stand face to face

With the dim heaven above,
And the eternal wrong he never could redress.
And she who seemed the shadow of his love,
   Risen from the graveyard green,
Passed, yet turned backward ere she passed,
     A lingering look to cast.
     She too had seen
The wedlock of their shadows, she had raised
Her eyes to his, had met a glance amazed—
An awestruck glance, that saw her golden head
Beautiful with the beauty of the dead—
    And in his startled eyes
Somewhat that startled her had leapt to light,
     Somewhat of pride
Made an imperious claim that would not be denied—
Somewhat of pain and wrong, unspoken, dim,
Looked forth, and drew her pity down to him.
A feeling that she scarce could recognise
Awoke within her, snatched a white disguise
Of prayer and thrilling with a strange affright,
Followed him through the shadows of the night.

EPILOGUE.

These shadows of an unknown land and age
Passing afar upon their pilgrimage,
Fell for a little space across my page.

A shadow hand lay side by side with mine,
And ever as I wrote it penned a line
Whose purport I but dimly can divine.

Too faint, too subtle ; yet if any read
My dream, half spoiled in writing, I would plead
'The shadow lines, between my verses, heed !'

There is so much that I have failed to say—
The dusky figures, gliding on their way,
Elude me, and the light of every day

Comes, slowly widening o'er the world again—
I look for all my midnight crowd in vain,
Gone ! and the written words alone remain.

Out of the shadows of an unknown night
The vision came.   A momentary light
Revealed the crowding shapes in hurried flight.

Even as they fled they sorrowed and embraced,
Across the narrow gleam I saw them haste
Into the shadows where no path is traced.

I have no word to answer should you ask
Their further fortunes—not for me the task
To follow them and bid the End unmask.

When I can understand the scope and worth
Of but one deed of all deeds done on earth—
When I can trace it backward to its birth,

And onward, through whatever may befall,
Unto its end, then will I hear your call,
Question me then, and I will answer all.

Not now, for now with doubting steps I go
And in the peopled twilight dimly know
Strange marriage-bonds between things high and
  low.

Faint whispers in the woodlands and the streams,
Half-lights, uncertain shadows, wandering gleams,
A clouded sky, a wilderness of dreams.

Longing for light a little way I creep,
·And guard the thought that, when I fall asleep,
Others shall climb the never-conquered steep,

And see our pathways, trodden long before,
Lie far below them as a level floor ;
While vast horizons widen evermore,

—Yet evermore are girdled with a zone
Of dusky cloud, the land of things unknown,
Of days to come and days forespent and flown—

And man still climbing shall look up to meet
The light that draws him while his pulses beat,
Smiting all shadows downward to his feet.

But while the vision rises nobly fair,
A voice in every ripple of the air
Whispers of things that are not, though they were.

A voice of changing seasons, changing times,
From often trodden ways, and far-off climes,
With dying echoes woven into rhymes.

' Idly you wander—whither leads your way ?
You watch the shadows—are you not as they ?
They pass and are forgotten—shall you stay ?

' Have you not listened to the summer breeze,
And listening, dreamed, beneath the leafy trees,
Of sunsets, dying over unknown seas,

Of dawn, far off and fair on sovereign heights,
Or keenest splendour of unresting lights
In the great loneliness of northern nights—

'Of white waves breaking on a desert beach,
Unseen, unknown, unuttered in your speech,
Unseen, unknown, as far beyond your reach

'As fallen snow when come the summer rains,
As bygone sweetness of a wild bird's strains,
As jests and fancies, lost in dead men's brains?

'The lavish beauty dawns while no man heeds,
And, like the wind's quick whisper in the reeds,
It dies away, not measured by your needs,

'Beyond you, lost for ever! Will you say
That the great world rolls backward on its way
To bring again the grace of yesterday—

'Backward, to battle for the shattered spoil
That Death has hidden 'neath the trampled soil,
Backward, to seek with melancholy toil,

The flower that bloomed and dropped, the flame
    that died,
The song's last echo? No, in fruitful pride
It hastens onward, casting all aside.

'Fresh buds unclose where withered blossoms grew,
Fresh melodies ring out when skies are blue,
Nature is glad, and all the world is new.

'Since first the years in changing seasons ran
All grace and beauty live their little span,
Why not the beauty and the joy of man?

'Nature has never reached a hand to save,
Has never paused beside an open grave
To give again the life that once she gave.

'Shadows and men she sees them every one
Passing away, as pass when day is done
Black flights of birds across the western sun.'

So speaks the voice and pauses in its flow,
I answer, What am I that I should know?
Must all our life be quenched?   It may be so.

It may be so.   Yet can it change my cry?
Let the last man be nobler far than I
Though I am dead, though he shall surely die.

It may be so.   Yet who can tell the height,
The joy, the white perfection of the light
He may attain before the coming night?

Who knows what clearer vision there may be
In the great days that I shall never see ?
—Shall not this hope be hope enough for me ?

Why must a mortal love be meaner, less,
Nor rather rise on high, through narrowing stress,
To passion of all-giving tenderness ?

With other hearts our hearts must beat and ache,
Life were not much to give for their dear sake,
Life were not much to give, nor death to take.

Nay we may dream each planet has its dower,
Of hidden hope, and at the destined hour
Opens in sweet and solitary flower—

Burns in a glory of consuming fire,
Sudden and strong as passionate desire,
Then dies in ashes like a funeral pyre—

Breaks forth in song that soars with wingéd strain
To silver heights, transforming all its pain
To music—then the silence comes again.

If like a shadow, or a passing sigh,
Love, thus made perfect from the world must die,
Scorn it who will, I will not scorn it—I !

1878.

A SHADOW ON THE DIAL.

I am yet young. Yet am not I so young
But that along life's tense and fraying thread
Run sudden tremors—thoughts of age to come,
And of the final snapping, which is Death.
Each thrill a stab, and then a lingering ache ;
A note which startles—echoes, faints, and dies.
As if the quivering string made sad response
Unto a far-off hand ; upraised to warn
And smite, like that whereof the legend tells,
Which wrote in awful mercy on the wall.

Then do I dream of something which pursues,
With lengthened strides as years run shortened by.
A step 'mid blue-bells when they come again,
A step beneath June's canopy of green,
A sigh which wanders with the wandering wind,
A rustle mixed with autumn's rustling leaves,
A chill which falls with winter's falling snow.

Only a sigh, a shadow and a chill.
Not altogether pain—a bitterness
Which adds a last intensity to joy.
He know's Love's agony of rapture best,
Who hears, amid his lady's loving talk,
An echo from the regions of the grave ;
Who crops the blossoms of his life in haste
And flings them down before her, lest they fail
To share the death he sees upon her face.
Her face, his flower, or no ! his star—Ah God !
Too like a star, which, doomed in highest heaven,
Flames in unwonted splendour ere it dies !
And evermore, as hurrying years go round,
Is not June sweeter that December comes ?
And blossoms that they fade ?   Yes, better so.
For who would cherish an unfading flower,
With which a thousand other hands had toyed,
Whose petals scores of unknown lips had brushed ?
Now, lost, it dies, or lingers faintly pure,
Crowned with the hazy halo of a dream ;
But if it lived from June to June, the vile
Might wear your rose, or it might be the gift
Another lover gave another love.
Let the undying flowers we should profane
Bloom sacredly in sacred Paradise,
And leave the poorer garlands gathered here,
The sad, supreme, pathetic charm of death.

For Death is great, inscrutable, alone
Common to all, but never commonplace.
It overhangs our dull and hackneyed lives,
As the grey silence of an endless cliff,
Sheer to the flood, and towering to the sky,
Defies and dominates a waste of waves.
Death is a king, whose face we should behold
With awe, but not with loathing—Death is great.
Ah ! but Old Age, his herald !   See the bent
Decrepit messenger, who totters first
To lead us to his presence—clasps our hands
With shaking fingers, checks our fearless step,
Constraining it to his,—and leans on us,
Till, bowed and sickened with his hateful weight,
We crawl, half willingly, to meet our doom.

Idly I muse, and fashion pictures thus,
Yet age, meanwhile, to me is nothing, save
A chill, a shapeless shadow, and a sigh.
But in the coming days how shall it be ?
Then will the shadow take an awful shape ?
Then will the chill freeze all the springs of hope ?
Then will the sigh become a weary moan
Breathed from within, not wandering without ?
If so, fain would I look it in the face.
Who would not rather meet a spectral form

Fresh from the laughing circle of his friends,
Than in a vigil, where the meanest things
Loom through the shadows, strange and terrible ?

Come then, Old Age, and let me see your face.
Utter your spell, whereat the blood runs cold,
Bind mine, for sport, in brief and bitter frost,
—I smile, since it must flow unchecked again,—
Show me your pall, which, flung across the world,
Will settle slowly down in sable folds,
—My God will rend the gloomy veil for me.—
Are you so busy, darkening men's lives
In awful earnest, that there is no time
For jesting?   Needs must I resign the hope,
And yet it haunts me.   Would it might have been !
What harm if I had stood a vision's space,
And gathered thoughts, then with a mute farewell,
Gone on my journey towards our common goal ?
It may not be.   And I am left alone,
To grasp, and bring to light my lurking fear.

Dim eyes, dull ears, slow pulses, failing knees,
Hard, hard to bear, but these are not old age.
For say it pleased my God to strike me blind,
Make me a cripple, whose enfeebled life
Ebbs by the fireside,—am I therefore old ?

D

No ! for my sightless eyes will surely serve
For bursts of youthful weeping—' Blind ! and all
Is loveliness around me !   Paradise
Is the wide world, which I shall never see !
Godlike the strife which I shall never share ! '
Not mine the hopeless burden of old age,
' Ah ! once there was a world all golden-green,
Which since has withered to a dreary grey.
Great lives were lived, and strenuous battles fought —
Yes, those were men !   Now a degenerate mob
Hustle each other on a downward road ! '
Thus may my grandsire muse, across the rug,
Stare at the kettle, watch the cinders fall,
He in his easy chair, while I in mine
Feel sharper anguish,—joy compared to his.
I know I cannot win the Koh-i-noor,
He thinks his eyes are opened, and 'tis glass,
I am the richer, by the Koh-i-noor !

Youth—age—how does my fancy shape itself !
I seem to see an airy, vacant room,
With open casements, where the azure shines
Through leaflessness of interlacing boughs ;
Not bare, as when November's latest leaf
Has shivered sadly downward to the mire,
But leaflessness of March, a ruddy haze
Flushing the twigs with promise of the spring.

Shadows of branches waver on the floor,
And 'mid the wavering shadows plays a child,
And, like the shadows, flickers to and fro.
Now, at the wide bright windows, golden hair
Glistens in golden sunlight, and blue eyes
Search the blue vault, while the spring-scented breeze
Breaks in soft billows on his lifted face.
And now with small feet pattering on the boards,
He wakes the silent room to share his mirth.
Then sitting on the floor, in childish thought,
He tosses here and there a heap of flowers,
And, because all his life is only spring,
The crocus-cups, that overflow with spring,
To him are nought but playthings.   He is young,
And so it is he knows not he is young,
Nor any other old.   Wanton he tears
The blossoms into little saffron shreds,
And flings them down.   Who will, may piece the
    leaves,
And read their message innocently sweet.

    Just a tiny blue-eyed maid,
    Newly out of Eden strayed ;
    Lips, a bud rose-tinted, rare,
    And the sunlight in her hair—
        Here is Spring !

Leaves are few to make her bowers
Bunches bright of leafless flowers
Are by baby fingers placed
Side by side, in happy haste—
       Little Spring !

Gardens dark with winter gloom,
All at once begin to bloom ;
Budding branches, lifted high,
Laugh and whisper in the sky,
       'Welcome, Spring !'

She will reach their stately height—
What to her are blossoms bright?
Little Spring, in haste to pass,
Lets them fall among the grass—
       Eager Spring !

Tip-toe stands, with parted lips,
Cannot reach their swaying tips,
Brushes past in April grief—
See ! The underwood in leaf !
       Fairy Spring !

She is growing tall and slim,
And her eyes are darkly dim,

Deepening with the deepening sky,
Darkening with the blue-bell's dye,
    —Is it Spring?—

They were wide and undismayed,
Timid now, and veiled in shade--
Comes a sound of hurrying feet,
She is flushed with roses sweet—
    Happy Spring!

Ah! last moment here she stood.
Gone for ever! Through the wood
Came young Summer, and in bliss
Died she 'neath his burning kiss—
    Farewell, Spring!

Throw wide the windows to a golden flood
Of sunlight, song, and perfume,—June is here!
Now reigns the rose in pride of flower and leaf,
And drops the curtain of her tangled sprays,
Laden with blossom, o'er the grave of spring.
Now come strange thrills of impulse unto one
Who feels the early summer in his veins,
And finds all sweetness 'neath the arching blue,
Sweeter, because of one most sweet of all.
The earth is full of joy and melody,
Yet he looks upward, for the clouds unfold

The loveliness of visionary lands,
Bright in the airy silence of the sky.
He dreams of heights ascended—glorious toil,
And glorious recompense,—when kneeling crowds
Shall prove his worthiness to kneel to *her*,
And conquest show his right to serve mankind.
And other dreams he has that know no shape,
Since June has joys too delicate and vague
For human speech, joys that are subtly linked
To thoughts of her, beyond all utterance.
The summer world is fair, and she is fair,
She is his world, and all its beauty hers.

My Summer is a fair, triumphant queen,
Who on her joyous way, through glade and glen,
With song and dainty masque, in woodlands green,
        Makes glad the hearts of men,

So that they love the sunlight and the rose,
Smile, and forget their bitter wrongs and pains,
Gaze at her pageant, and the life-blood flows
        Rejoicing, through their veins.

When she is gone, all gladness will depart,
Slow dying—can I be content with this?
Not while my heart can seek the throbbing heart
        That floods the world with bliss !

So from her fleeting loveliness I fly,
Choosing the endless summer for my goal,
And hasten—all my soul a longing cry—
    To seek the summer's soul !

Look now upon a wilderness of wealth,
Of barren glitter, and bright mockery ;
Where blazonry is more than sky and stars,
And woven splendours from an eastern loom,
With perfumed folds shut out the breath of heaven.
Yet though the master of this shining hoard
Be ever watchful—stretching greedy hands
Unto far islands, and remotest shores,
And though he pile up treasure year by year,
—Computing time by growth of glittering heaps—
Among his jewels you shall never find
Spring's crocus gold, nor diamond dew of June.
The shadows gather fast, the night comes on,
And what is there can give him back his youth ?

Ah my God ! I lingered, stooping, in a dim and
    leafy place,
And my groping hand uncovered Autumn's wan
    discoloured face !
Then a sudden, sullen shiver ran and died among
    the trees,

And I see that face in all things, and I fly with
    trembling knees.
Fly—but whither? Days are shortened, and the leaves
    are falling fast—
I have not found the summer's soul, and all my hope
    is past !

One last look. All the air is close and faint,
And in the dimness of his curtained bed
He lies, worn out, and weary of his life ;
While round him come and go the busy throngs
That his dim eyes would follow if they could.

He has grown grey. Perhaps. He scarcely knows.
He almost fancies that the world is grey.
The joy of life is gone—'tis hardly pain,
But is there not a dull, unceasing ache
Throughout the universe? There was a time,
Happy, but long departed, when he deemed
That life, and joy, and energy, were one
And his for evermore. But now, is not
All nature growing feeble, and all life
Low in the socket? Well, the joyous past
Is past, and comes no more. Nought but to wait
Till this be also past. How long? How long ?
No longer. Suddenly the thread is snapped.

God looks upon him with His face of Death,
And lifts him up to learn that God is Life.

O the great breath he draws !   The startled gaze !
God's sky *is* sapphire, then !   God's earth is green !
Gone are the sullen clouds—Decay and Age,
Dim spectral tyrants, fled into the past.
Henceforth no death—life only—death is nought.
No darkness, but a shoreless sea of light—
Nor youth, nor age, but God is all in all.

Thus in my fancy runs the course of life,
And murmurs, as it flows through sun and shade,
' Never look back to yearn for what is past.'
Youth is not in the days when we were young,
Nor in the places which we loved when young ;
Given to our longing, we should find them old,
Empty, and meaningless.   O foolish hearts !
Never so young as when our straining eyes
Look for a future which shall crown us kings ;
Never so old as when we dream of youth,
And long for it—a thing apart and gone.

So a man lingers on a mountain range,
And, loath to go, looks downward from his height
Upon a sunset lake of lucid fire,

Which lies amid its banks of ruddy cloud.
He stands and gazes, till his heart is stirred,
Drawn to the glory, yearning to possess
Light, and the glowing hues, and splendid calm.
Yet with a sudden sigh he turns away,
Fronts the cold blankness of the far-off East,
And passes slowly downward, to the sad
And shrouded wilderness of vales below.
Gone is the widespread beauty of the world,
For step by step the summits shut him in ;
Crags overhang his ever-narrowing path,
And beneath every crag and every tree
Lurks Night, to spring upon the shrinking Dusk.
Weary and chilled is he—the pathway rough,
He stumbles onward, but his thoughts go back
To the bright glory of the western sky,
The tranquil height, the warm and golden air,
The blue above, the sunny turf below—
His thoughts go back, but still he stumbles on.

Darkness, and cloud, and bitter driving rain—
What matter ? For his face is toward the east,
And his shall be the dawning of the day.
The greyness of old age is but a mist
From the dark valley where our graves are dug ;
A chilly vapour, which obscures the world

And hides from us the sun's bright certainty,
Till all is dim, and, could we so resist
God's onward impulse, we should struggle back
To search the western heaven for the dawn !
Nay, urge us forward, Lord, and bid us win
Thy orient flower of white and perfect day !

But if I thus believe, why fear old age ?
Why not pass boldly through the mocking mist,
In full assurance of eternal youth,
And of the final triumph of the sun?
Ah ! but my faith is like the sun itself—
No little talisman to have and hold,
And grasp more tightly when the shadows come ;
But a mysterious majesty of light,
Across whose glory billows of black cloud
Drive, and the sudden darkness is astir
With wavering of fantastic shapes of doubt.
Unto the very verge of death we go
With those who die.   We meet their failing eyes,
And we are sad—not seeing how that look
Of unbelief shall rise to breathless awe,
And, as the golden light succeeds the grey,
Shall brighten to an ecstasy of peace—
And so there is a shadow on the end.
Here, plain enough, the sombre threads of life,

Twisted and tangled in a sullen maze ;
And overhead—O surely overhead
Shine through earth's clouds of dust the golden
        strings
Of lives, which, set in heaven as in a harp,
Pour forth their flood of melody on high.
Surely we hear—Nay, who will make us sure ?
From the dim distance to this warring world,
The music comes so faint and fitfully,
—Clamour and moans on this side and on that—
We lean and listen, drawing down our brows,
And sometimes lose, and sometimes half believe.
O if some sudden trumpet note might peal,
So that the world a moment held its breath
Amazed, and then, uplifting a great voice,
—The utterance of its countless multitudes—
Joined in the strain, and made the gathering notes
As thunder—then an overflowing stream—
A great flood irresistible—and last,
A steady, upward rush of wings to God !

Too fair a dream for hope ! We must go on,
Must journey through the miry ways of earth,
And labour in its shadows, to the end.
Ever the changeless change of day and night
Continues, noon and twilight, gloom and glow

There comes no blaze of dazzling certainty
To flood the world, and drown each dim recess
In waves of living light.   Too fair the dream !
Too blinding bright, too terrible the boon !

God give me strength to journey steadfastly
Unto the East, nor miss the wayside gift
Of leaf and song.   O that my heart may beat
For coming life, and for the hurried clash
Of the world's march, yet never lose the tunes,
Tender and sweet, to which old days were set !
Still, as years fleet, may every crocus cup
O'erflow for me with the new wine of spring;
Still let me love the morning's dewy calm,
The wind that whispers of the far-off waves,
The hum of bees, the daisies in the grass,
The music all the little brooks pour forth
To while away their weary course, until
They meet the boundless welcome of the sea;
Still may my soul be glad among the flowers,
Thrill to the sun's warm kisses on the dew,
And rise, renewed, in freshness after rain.

Yet not such joy alone—the pain too, Lord,
The special suffering of this special age,
Give me my portion of its bitter cup.

I shrink from it, yet, being what I am,
I were not greater than my fellow men,
But meaner, less, if while they bowed their backs
'Neath weary loads, or hewed an upward path,
I, steeped in idle happiness, should gaze
With half-closed eyes, that scarcely care to see.
I would not take the flowers, and leave to them
The nobler share, the sweat-drops of their toil.
Give me youth's highest right—nay, very youth
Itself, the knowledge that my every pulse
Beats with the inmost pulses of the age ;
And that not only in its hours of hope;
Not only in its victories and joys—
Give labouring sobs, to match the labouring sob
Wrung from a toiling world—defiant cry
Of battle, in the lurid times of war—
Yearnings for guidance in the days of doubt;
For through such sympathy, in suffering,
In hope, in triumph, quickened into life,
I gain a glimpse of something more than joy,
Higher than rapture, distant as a star—
A time beyond all time—a steadfast gaze—
An ever-widening thought—when my weak heart,
Lifted above self-consciousness, shall beat
In unison with His, unchangeable,
Who, through the rolling ages, says I AM.

O star of hope ! The beating wings of time
Droop, wearied, fail my longing, and thou art
Perfect as ever, and as ever, far.
Yet, wert thou quenched, the heavens were black
  indeed !

I end as I began.   Through gliding days
I watch the spinning of the thread of life,
Which lengthens, lengthens even as I write,
And thrills with meaning to its utmost length.
My path before me glimmers through the grey,
I rise, and follow it.   Though shadows come,
And drifting vapours darken into night—
Though fear arise, and front me as despair—
Here stands the record of my happier faith.

It stands, but I go forward, will be brave
To bear, to toil—Ah God ! the icy doubt !
How will it be when life is burning dim,
In evil days when hope and joy are dead ?
Lord, if Thy signals grow but faint and few,
Give me assurance that they are from Thee,
The Life of Life, flowing in perfect strength,
Not weakened—all the imperfection mine.
Then send Thy final message—a white flash
To snap the thread, and light me to Thy feet !

1873.

THE LEVEL LAND.[1]

STIRRED by great aims, our eager souls leap high
As flame, or living tree, or slender tower;
But withered longings round such life must lie,
Fallen like flowers of spring foredoomed to die,
After a little space of sun and shower.
Our trodden world is touched with poets' fire;
Star-like, unknown, there hangs a world above;
And we have life, can labour and aspire,
And seek for God; yet sometimes I desire—
Ah! how desire a level land I love!

A land of sunny turf and laughing rills,
A land of endless summer, sweet with dew,
Girt with a range of everlasting hills,
Asleep beneath a sky of white and blue.
There, with a silver flash, 'mid grove and lawn,
Like curving blades are thrust the narrow creeks,
And ocean breezes rush at dusk and dawn
With songs of freedom round the guardian peaks.

[1] First published in *Harper's Magazine* for November 1880.

In sparkling air the poplars quiver high;
In every thicket sing the birds unseen;
O'er sculptured walls, beneath the glowing sky,
Fruits cluster, purple-ripe; and waters lie
Lucid in fountains rimmed with mossy green.

A clearer music whispers in the reeds
Than reeds have ever learned by brooks of ours,
And throughout all the year the level meads
Are golden-green, and sprinkled full of flowers.
As some dear child once more at home might stand,
Her very self, but taller and more fair—
Herself, yet changed in eyes and brow and hair—
So like, unlike, the flowers in that far land,
And violets grow very thickly there.

And there is many a wide and busy way
Which echoes with the singing of sweet words
And greetings ; for the wayfarers are gay,
Light, and unwearied as the darting birds.
Their eyes are glad for beauty that has been,
Glad for new beauty, where they feast afresh.
And every face is delicate and keen,
Clothed but not burdened with its garb of flesh.
Nor is among them stammering thought nor tongue,
But eyes and lips and hands have perfect speech.

E

Outlines, or mingled hues, words said or sung,
Sweet wordless looks, and music finely strung
Belong to all, and answer each to each.

Maidens are there might bid a gazer deem
That the soft shadows of the eventide—
The balmy dusk when day has newly died—
Flowed in their veins, a swift and subtle stream,
So darkly sweet among the flowers they glide.
Their garments, as they flit between the trees,
Blend their rich dyes in one imperial glow,
Like a fair garden of anemones
When blossoms open and the south winds blow.
And others look upon that land's delight,
Grey-eyed and stately—women queenly souled—
Golden their hair, and in their raiment white
Have cunning fingers woven flowers of gold.

They have no laughter there of lofty scorn,
Nor of a gladness from the world apart,
No sidelong merriment, no satire born
Of hidden pain and weariness of heart.
Joy of the world with joy of man unites—
Gladness of brooks that glitter in the sun,
Greetings of lovers, leafy shades and lights
Dancing in golden riot, all are one.

Sweet with the kiss of ripples on the sand,
With mirth of flower and bird, of maid and boy,
Goes up the laughter of the level land,
Its clearest note the note of human joy.

Like a midsummer madrigal which tells
Of golden love in notes like golden bells
Is that fair land for which I vainly long;
And even were I throned where gladness dwells,
Mine were a note of discord in the song.
For dim perplexities, and hopes that wane,
Doubt, and the ghastly riddles Sin and Pain,
Burden of Duty, and contending creeds,
Would still pursue, oppress my weary brain,
And mar the music of the river reeds.

O heavy Thought! Can Sleep no comfort yield,
Who conquers every pain with transient health—
Lost ere the sick heart knew that it was healed—
Fair Sleep, who mocks and blesses us by stealth,
Bids us be kings and rule the empty air,
Fly on swift pinions, or renew our youth—
Can Sleep no comfort yield in my despair?
O for a sleep whose visions, faint and fair,
Should gather strength, should win a virtue rare,
Open like buds, and blossom into Truth!

Is there such perfect slumber 'neath the sky?
Nay, is there not?   It might be found, I think,
Could I attain that land.   Could I but lie
Upon the level turf, and softly sigh,
'Mid the soft sighing of the water's brink,
Till I forgot the strife of Right and Wrong,
Forgot the gloom of overhanging Death,
And slept off all my care 'mid rippling song,
Might I not rise, and drawing fuller breath,
Wake to no torpid creeping of the blood,
But a quick rush of life—no languid flow
Of joy wrung out amid encircling woe,
But gladness pouring in a golden flood?
Dream of a fool!   The soul makes answer, No.

Not mine, nor shall be mine from first to last,
That level land.   There rises from the sod—
O glory inconceivable and vast!
Awful as fate, and silent as the past—
Dimly, an infinite ascent to God.

Not mine that land, in days afar or near.
How could I ever long its shores to win?—
I who strain upward toward an atmosphere
Of sovereign calm, so thin and crystal clear
All lower life must faint and die therein.

Yet is my path encompassed by the spell.
It lurks in written page and carven stone,
And blossoms from our laboured gardens tell
Of fair lands golden-crowned with asphodel,
Where joys and flowers spring up, alike unsown.
What marvèl if at times I dream again,
When earth is warm, and heaven is blue above,
And yearning for that vision sweet and vain,
Shrink from the soul's high heritage of pain?
O land—fair land! O level land I love!

OUT OF THE DARKNESS.

NIGHT.

THE tardy night is here.   I welcome it,
Since darkness makes me, for a little while
Fair as my fellow-girls.   These eyes alone,—
On which my form is branded as with fire—
Can see me, now the world is blind with night
And hushed in heavy sleep.   I would there were
No morning light to throw a covering shape,
Distorted past distortion, on the wall !

I am alone.   I think there is no girl
Who would not shudder, were she left alone
With such deformity, in doubtful night,
Who, flying from the horror, would not claim
Your pity.   But my shuddering loneliness
Lasting so long outlasts all sympathy.
The golden cord, as strong as loving arms,

With which compassion girds us in our pain
And holds us up, is drawn through lengthened years
To gossamer, that on the summer air
Drifts uselessly, and all unheeded, breaks.

Now is the time, when, kneeling by their beds,
Girls pray in whispers, gentle faces bowed
Upon their folded hands.   And while their lips
Pause, ere a name be uttered, they may glide
Unwittingly, from prayer to reverie,
Then waken with a start, all rosy-red
With shame and tenderness, as if they stayed
To clasp fond hands upon the narrow way
And found their backs were turned on Paradise !
If a stray thought of me should cross their minds
Would they not pity me ?   Yet they would say
'Surely her prayers are purer far than ours,
Untroubled by these sweetly wilful dreams.
No eager eyes meet hers, to draw aside
Her upward gaze, no softly lingering words
Will fill her ears with music, when at night
She listens, till the Spirit shall say, Come.
'Tis hard for us to put the joy aside ;
But she—now shall she not win heaven, who needs
Must scorn the world?   How shall she not embrace
God's love, to whom the love of man is nought ?'

To whom the love of man is nought ! O fools !
It is for that I moan in blackest night.
My soul is burning in a quenchless thirst
For love. My fancy roams through endless dreams,—
Known all the time for sickening emptiness—
Dreams, still of love. O for a word, one word !—
Yet every word is like a stinging lash,
Pity or insult, both are agony !
For one fond touch—yet every touch is fire !
Nothing but human eyes can give the love
I die for—eyes that brand me when they glance !
Thus evermore I moan in blackest night.

Were I a poet I might acquiesce
In this accursed burden of the flesh,
Lie crushed and quiet, while my song uprose
And rang above the heads of stately men
And fairest women, bidding them look up
Unto my dreams, more fair and stately still.
I too might lift my eyes, and see myself,
As they would see me, soaring high as heaven.
Had I such wings I might afford to scorn
The ugliness that no one then would heed.
When, in the final hour of swaying fight,
The trumpet notes ring keen through ear and soul,
Who stops to cavil at the trumpet's form ?

But here am I, misshapen, slow of speech,
Having within me, for my only gift,
The woman's power of answering love with love.
O mockery ! I read it in the eyes,
The searching, scorching eyes that madden me !
Why was not I a creature born to fight?
Born to give hate for loathing? That were well.
But here lies, helplessly, a human heart
Which every careless passer-by may spurn,
A human heart that aches in blackest night.

'Morbid !' the world protests. 'This anguish looms
Large, through the mist of your distempered dreams.
Some mock at you no doubt, but mockery   .
Is mostly want of thought. And many a glance
Looks kindlier on you, for sweet pity's sake,
And lingers gently. Why will you repulse
Such glances ?'

       I am parched with thirst for love,
And do you bid me quench my thirst with this
The shattered spray of love's out-pouring tide,
Only a scanty dew, the niggard shower
Of pity, spared from love, and never missed !
Shall I drink this? I say it mocks my lips—
It is not pity that I need, but love !

Vainly I make my moan in blackest night.
Again the world comes in ' Love God ! Love God ! '
Why should I love Him, since He loves not me,
Nor ever cared to teach me how to love,
By perfect love of any soul on earth?
He is Omnipotent—a cripple I.
It may be that hereafter He will show
Love in despite of this—but can He ask
That I should read His love in very wrong?
It may be.   Yet I know not.   This I know,
That I am daily learning how to hate,
With deadliest hatred, born of love repulsed !—
But if thus warped in heart I were to find
Another woman, tortured like myself,
And felt within my soul the smallest gift
Of help, I could not hold my hand, my hate
Could never reach such height of cruelty
As can this love of God—if it be love,
And not a cold, supreme, eternal scorn.

' Nay, but the Christ' you say ' Who leans from
        heaven,
The Man of sorrows, stretching wounded hands,
To clasp and hold the hands of sorrowing men,
Christ who was scourged, and mocked and crucified,
Christ, like yourself, rejected and despised,

Enthrone Him in your heart, your Lord and Love,
And you shall have no need of love of man.

Vainly you plead.   I look, but answer No.
If I were fair enough for men to seek
It might be I could put their love aside
To choose the mystic Bridegroom, clasp that sweet
Eternal, yearning, melancholy Love,
And keep a white virginity for Him.
Not now.   I will not give for sacrifice
That which all men deride ; nor offer dumb
Endurance, as submission to God's will ;
Nor loathèd loneliness for chastity !

Talk not of Christ—what is your Christ to me ?
Rejected, scorned—O easy scorn to bear !
Let millions mock, if here and there a heart
Carries its love for you through all the years,
Nay if but one were faithful, that were all.
One heart may be a world.   A world !   One heart
May hold the meaning of the universe
Revealed to loving eyes.   But as for me,
What is your Christ to me ?   Look on that face,—
Pressed like a signet on the souls of men—
See where he stands, a dreamer, prophet, king,
Half feminine, but with a something else

Which being hardly human, may be God.
See little children crowd around his knees,—
The children who would scream in fear and hate
At sight of me !—Look on him where he sits
At his last supper, sought by ardent eyes
That swear devotion, while the man he loves
Leans on his bosom—Not till earth denied
Some hunted wretch a moment's resting place,
Would head be ever laid on heart of mine !—
See him once more, with sunlight and blue air
Around him, and the lilies at his feet—
See the great multitude stand hushed, intent
To lose no syllable of pleading love—
See—He stands up and speaks—and crouching, I
Stammer defiant hatred in the dark !

Go, preach your Christ, rejected and despised
'Mid those to whom the words are meaningless.
Preach your All-loving and Almighty God
To those He blesses.   As for me, I pray
To one God only—black Forgetfulness !

MORNING

It was a dream !   The daylight, pitiless,
Comes like a murderer !   A dreary streak
Stabs through the parted curtains, and the night
Grows pale, and dies.   O would to God that I
Could blind the hateful sun that glares on me
And blot him from the sky, for he has slain
The sweetest dream that soul has ever known.

God ! Give me death ! Or give me back my dream !
The cruel sun has killed it, and I live
To mourn it endlessly beneath his eye,—
My dream that blossomed in the loving night !
There is no shade in all the sultry world
And I shall never find my joy again.
Shut out the sunlight, let me press my face
Upon the pillow where I slept, and pray.—
For I believe there is a God who loves !

Last night I flung myself upon my bed
Bitter, and sick at heart.   Sleep kissed my eyes
And I was walking in an unknown land.
It was no garden, rich with fabled fruit,

No wondrous, dragon-haunted paradise,
But a wide harvest plain of tawny gold,
A glad and fruitful cornland.　Overhead
An arch of purple heaven, unclouded, still,
Bent to the far horizon ; in the west
It met a shadowy line of purple sea,
But, looking towards the dawn, no eye could part
The ripened yellow from the saffron light.

Tranquil and deep there lay a chain of pools
Full to the brim, like wine-cups at a feast.
All darkly pure they slumbered, and their glass
Was thinly sown with white and starlike buds
Of sleeping lilies.　Rushes' tufted spears
Stood round their margins, but no shadowing tree
Hung over them.　Between them and the height
Was nought, and each one held the solemn sky.

It was an unknown hour, a world unknown.
Perhaps it was the hush before the dawn,
For all the air was calm, and dewy sweet.
It might be, yet the orient crocus flame
Changed not, not yielded to the glaring day,
But kept its tender charm—as if a slim
Boy-herald, golden-haired, and saffron-clad,
Stood on the eastern threshold, but forgot

His errand, leaned to look with poet-eyes,
And feared to wake the land that was so still.

No reapers reaped in the upstanding corn,
No women gleaned, no little children sought
The poppies, flaunting 'mid the ripened ears.
No swift birds flew across the purple heaven,
No burnished flies skimmed o'er the dusky pools,
No light breeze stirred the myriad golden stalks,
Nor roused a ripple.   There was nought that moved
In that fair country but my love and I.

My love !   Come back to me, my vanished love,
Out of the vanished night !   My widowed hands
Seek yours in vain, and all the world is blank
Because I cannot find—No ! not your eyes !
Spare me that torture, Heaven !—I seek you not !
O God ! he could not love me 'neath the sun !

Yet how we loved beneath that purple sky,
Slow moving through the silent plain of gold,
Passing the waveless waters.   There we paused,—
A pause like that a skilled musician makes,
Which in itself is music and delight—
And gazed upon their depths.   A moment they
Mirrored my love, fit form for such a heaven !

I envied them their bliss, until our eyes
Met in a smile that filled my soul with peace.
I did not long to see my image there ;
There was no need, since he had smiled on me ;
And through his eyes I saw my loveliness,
Knew myself graceful as the ripened corn,
Pure as the dewy air, and fairer far
Than lilies on the dusky purple pools.
Ah, how we loved !   And yet we were not one,
For he was not myself, though not apart,
But as it were an inner soul of mine,
A new and nobler life within my own.

I scarcely think our voices broke the spell
Of that sweet silence.   Much he spoke to me,
But uttered it in swifter, finer wise
Than through the clumsy help of groping words,
So that I rather heard with heart than ear,
How he, through lonely life, in love with Love,
Found none on whom to lavish all the love
That ached within him, till, beside the pools,
He looked into my eyes, and on his soul
There sank a perfect stillness of content.

Was there no music in that golden land ?
I think the music and the land were one.

The pools which shadowed in their shadowy tide
The far and purple height, were yearning strains,

The arching heaven had solemn harmony.
The happy cornland sang of fruitful joy.
I looked upon my love—his perfect face
So darkly soft upon the saffron sky,
Was music of exceeding tenderness.
And as we wandered onward, side by side,
Our bodies, fair, and free and nobly poised,
Swayed in the sweetest rhythm, each to each,
An endless love song.   Music there was none
That quivers in the strings of lute and harp,
Rings clearly out from silver trumpet throat
Or breathes in passion of a singer's voice—
No little gushing rills of melody,
Which flow awhile, then cease.   But we had come
Unto the fount and well-spring of all music ;
Unfathomed, unprofaned, eternal, full,
And therefore still, but music's very soul :

How shall I tell the ending of my dream ?

A luckless wretch was pent, they say, for years
Within a dungeon.   Unto him, unmanned,
Despairing, weak, a great deliverance came.
He knew not how he passed the watchful guards,

And gained his freedom ; but he staggered forth
Into the happy world of trees and flowers.
He felt the grass beneath his feet, the air
Upon his face, the sky above his head,
God over all.　He could not even think
That he was free—was free !—but drunk with bliss,
Rushed onward in a rapture, just to meet
His gaoler, duly warned, and waiting him,
Not angry, not alarmed, but with a smile
Lurking about his mouth, and in his eyes,—
And all the dungeon in that quiet smile !
How, think you, felt that thunderstricken dupe?
Was it as I felt, when the mocking sun
Stared in my face, and all my dream was dead?

My love is gone !　Gone my one glimpse of joy !
My doom is still upon me !　I must wear
This hideous mask, and with misshapen limbs
Drag my dull burden—hide in darkest holes—
Hunted for ever by the laughing light
That looked upon my love and murdered him !

But I am not the same.　You see no change,
And yet I am new born since yesternight.
Born to new anguish, to a longing love,
To endless yearning at the core of life,

To pain so exquisite, so keen, so dear,
Not for one moment would I let it go
Out of my heart.   And, clasping it, I scorn
The coarser joys that pass for happiness
With those who never knew a dream like mine!

Narrow and dull and hopeless is the world,
But in my soul I hide the crocus light
Of that unchanging dawn.   And O my love !
Slain by the sunlight, evermore you live
Within the mournful shadows of my life,
And all the dusk is dear for your dear sake.
O love of mine !   You taught me how to weep,
Teaching me how to love you, and my tears
Have more than sweetness in their bitter salt !

Even my dungeon world is not the same,
For it may vanish, as it vanished then,
Perhaps for ever.   And I have a thought—
Almost a hope—that when in God's good time
The world shall greet its latest dawn, He may
Remember me.   His heaven—so say the priests—
Means multitudes, and victory, and joy,
One life of rapture in a myriad souls.
But—since on earth I lived so long apart,
That to my mind a crowd can mean but pain,

Torture, and loneliness—I think, perhaps,
That when His countless saints triumphantly
Rejoice around Him, He may look aside,
And let the two, on whom He smiled last night,
Slip out of all the splendour and the song,
To walk together 'neath the purple sky,
Beside the lilied pools, and through the corn,
In the melodious silence of my dream.

But, if that may not be, O let me keep
Remembrance to the last !   Have mercy, God
Nor heal me of the pain that is my soul ! '

February 1875.

A JAPANESE FAN.[1]

How time flies ! Have we been talking
    For an hour?
Have we been so long imprisoned
    By the shower
In this old oak-panelled parlour?
    Is it noon?
Don't you think the rain is over
    Rather soon?

Since the heavy drops surprised us,
    And we fled
Here for shelter, while it darkened
    Overhead ;
Since we leaned against the window,
    Saw the flash
Of the lightning, heard the rolling
    Thunder crash ;

[1] First published in the *Cornhill Magazine* for September 1876.

You have looked at all the treasures
    Gathered here,
Out of other days and countries
    Far and near ;
At those glasses, thin as bubbles,
    Opal bright—
At the carved and slender chessmen
    Red and white—
At the long array of china
    Cups and plates—
(Do you really understand them ?
    Names and dates ?)
At the tapestry, where dingy
    Shepherds stand,
Holding grim and faded damsels
    By the hand,
All the while my thoughts were busy
    With the fan
Lying here—bamboo and paper
    From Japan.
It is nothing—very common—
    Be it so ;
Do you wonder why I prize it ?
    Care to know ?
Shall I teach you all the meaning,
    The romance

Of the picture you are scorning
    With a glance ?

From Japan ! I let my fancy
    Swiftly fly ;
Now if we set sail to-morrow,
    You and I,
If the waves were liquid silver,
    Fair the breeze,
If we reached that wondrous island
    O'er the seas,
Should we find that every woman
    Was so white,
And had slender upward eyebrows
    Black as night ?
Should we then perhaps discover
    Why, out there,
People spread a mat to rest on
    In mid air ?

Here's a lady, small of feature,
    Narrow-eyed,
With her hair of ebon straightness
    Queerly tied ;
In her hand are trailing flowers
    Rosy sweet,

And her silken robe is muffled
      Round her feet.
She looks backward with a conscious
      Kind of grace,
As she steps from off the carpet
      Into space ;
Though she plants her foot on nothing
      Does not fall,
And in fact appears to heed it
      Not at all.
See how calmly she confronts us
      Standing there—
Will you say she is not lovely ?
      Do you dare ?
I will not !   I honour beauty
      Where I can,
Here's a woman one might die for !
      —In Japan.

Read the passion of her lover—
      All his soul
Hotly poured in this fantastic
      Little scroll.
See him swear his love, and vengeance
      Read his fate —

You don't understand the language ?
    I'll translate.

' Long ago,' he says, ' when summer
    Filled the earth
With its beauty, with the brightness
    Of its mirth ;
When the leafy boughs were woven
    Far above ;
In the noonday I beheld her,
    Her—my love !
Oftentimes I met her, often
    Saw her pass,
With her dusky raiment trailing
    On the grass.
I would follow, would approach her,
    Dare to speak,
Till at last the sudden colour
    Flushed her cheek.
Through the sultry heat we lingered
    In the shade ;
And the fan of pictured paper
    That she swayed
Seemed to mark the summer's pulses,
    Soft and slow,

And to thrill me as it wavered
    To and fro.
For I loved her, loved her, loved her,
    And its beat
Set my passion to a music
    Strangely sweet.

Sunset came, and after sunset
    When the dusk
Filled the quiet house with shadows ;
    And the musk
From the dim and dewy garden
    Where it grows,
Mixed its perfume with the jasmine
    And the rose;
When the western splendour faded,
    And the breeze
Went its way, with good-night whispers
    Through the trees,
Leaning out we watched the dying
    Of the light,
Till the bats came forth with sudden
    Ghostly flight.
They were shadows, wheeling, flitting
    Round my joy,

While she spoke and while her slender
    Hands would toy
With her fan, which as she swayed it
    Might have been
Fairy wand, or fitting sceptre
    For a queen.
When she smiled at me, half pausing
    In her play,
All the gloom of gathering twilight
    Turned to day !

Though to talk too much of heaven
    Is not well—
Though agreeable people never
    Mention hell—
Yet the woman who betrayed me—
    Whom I kissed—
In that bygone summer taught me
    Both exist.
I was ardent, she was always
    Wisely cool,
So my lady played the traitor,
    I—the fool '——
Oh, your pardon ! But remember,
    If you please,

I'm translating—this is only
    Japanese.

'Japanese?' you say, and eye me
    Half in doubt;
Let us have the lurking question
    Spoken out.
Is all this about the lady
    Really said
In that little square of writing
    Near her head?
I will answer, on my honour,
    As I can,
Every syllable is written
    On the fan.
Yes, and you could learn the language
    Very soon—
Shall I teach you on some August
    Afternoon?

You are wearied. There is little
    Left to say;
For the disappointed hero
    Goes his way,
And such pain and rapture never
    More will know.

But he smiles—all this was over
  Long ago.
I am not a blighted being—
  Scarcely grieve—
I can laugh, make love, do most things
  But believe !

Yet the old days come back strangely
  As I stand
With the fan she swayed so softly
  In my hand.
I can almost see her, touch her,
  Hear her voice,
Till, afraid of my own madness,
  I rejoice
That beyond my help or harming
  Is her fate—
Past the reach of passion—is it
  Love—or hate ?

This is tragic ! Are you laughing ?
  So am I !
Let us go—the clouds have vanished
  From the sky.
Yes, and you'll forget this folly ?
  Time it ceased,

For you do not understand me
In the least.
You have smiled and sighed politely
Quite at ease,—
And my story might as well be
Japanese !

THE UNKNOWN LAND.

F. WALKER. FEB. 12, 1876.

THE unknown land
Rises, in very truth, before their eyes—
    A land which long has been
    Desired, although unseen,
Unseen, unknown, and yet a strong desire !
    An unknown land,
Whereof dim visions floated through their sleep,
An unknown land, beyond an unknown deep—
    Now within reach it lies,
And drawn, and over-mastered by their prize,
With eager faces, and with souls on fire,
    They look on their desire.

    It is so near
That, as the boat glides landward, they can hear

The sweet lip-greeting of the sea,
The whisper, softly strong, of waters on the shore ;
    A music old
    Of murmurs manifold
Yet holding somewhat never heard before.
Near—nearer yet—the land where they would be,
    It is so near
    That Hope is almost Fear.

    It lies within their reach—
    The joy they crave—
    Their boat has touched the beach,
They wade in sudden coolness of the wave,
Which draws them in its tumult of retreat,
    Sucking the tawny sand
    From 'neath their feet.
There is a pause—the ocean pulses beat—
    Then flows the tide above the knee,
And, quickened by the heart-throb of the sea,
Sweeps those who long, yet waver where they stand,
With one vast impulse towards the unknown land.

What shall be theirs in this triumphant hour ?—
The folded bud of longing, faint at heart,
    Bursts into starry flower,
Crowning a day, from other days apart—

What shall be theirs within their new domain ?
What valleys, cloven in the fertile earth—
 What wondrous birth
Of blossom, garlanding the unknown ways—
What snow-fed torrents, leaping to the plain—
 What rocky hills that hold
 Great veins of virgin gold,
As hearts hold memories of golden days
 Gone by—
What unimagined glories in the sky—
 What music of strange words—
 What melody of birds
 That pipe and sing,
A-quiver, 'mid the green leaves quivering—
 What joy of liberty is there—
 What wide and unpolluted air,
 In this new land, where everything
Is full of hope, and wonderful, and fair !

Yet, even while they lean, with lips apart,
 And yearning eyes,
In stillness, 'neath the beating of each heart,
 Lie hidden memories,
That make no sign, but, as a sleeper lies
Alive, through death-like slumber, so they rest
 In every breast—

G

Thoughts of a far-off home, 'neath other skies,
Memories of a land of memories.

A land where plain and hill
Bear record still
Of triumph or defeat, in days gone by ;
A land that lies amid encircling waves,
Where multitudes of men are born and die ;
A land of many cities, great and proud,
A land of many graves.
The busy craftsmen crowd
Its trodden ways ; the plough, with yearly toil,
Makes furrows in the often-furrowed soil ;
And many an orchard close
Blossoms in white and rose,
When joyous May comes round
Again, and yet again,
And little children play upon the ground
Beneath a snowy rain
Of drifting petals, by the breezes strewn.
The summer sunlight falls
On red and massive walls,
Built long ago—
The happy birds take up the summer's tune,
And tottering folk, whose work in life is done,
Sit in the sun,

Where roses blow,
And watch the scythe, that, sweeping to and fro,
  Lays low
The ripened grass of June.

Even the flowers in that historic land,
    To dreaming fancy seem to stand
    In order ranged ;
Waiting the seasons' call to take their part
In sweetest masking, year by year unchanged,
    And known by heart.
    Clad in their festival array,
    These pretty players lift the head,
Utter the words of poets long since dead,
    And pass away.

Birds, woods, and waters, known and loved, have each
    Their human speech
Of softest cadence, and transfigured rise
In pictured grace, that we may recognise
    The loveliness supreme
    Revealed to painters' eyes.
    And one who dwelt within this land,
And found new beauty in its blossoms white,
    New joy in field and stream ;
And added by the labour of his hand

Unto its hoarded treasure of delight—
    Passing beyond our sight,
Has left a sketch like this, to bid us muse and dream.

    But even as we stand
Before his work, and with a lingering gaze
    Give him our grief for praise,
We wonder—has he found the Unknown Land?
And, dead to us, is he yet living there?
    Do all these memories to him
    Seem shadows, colourless and dim?
    Does he look back, as one who knows
The joy of June, the reddening of the rose,
Looks back to March with all its bitter days—
    As one who breathing summer air
Beneath the woven shade of leafy sprays
    With crimson buds aglow,
Thinks for a moment of the sprinkled snow
Of blackthorn blossom on the branches bare?
    Does he think thus
Of all his work that is so fair to us?

We cannot tell. The never-resting stream,
    Drawn towards a fate unseen,
    Glides onward like a dream
    For evermore.

We know not what its rippling whispers mean,
    Nor if its final wave
Breaks in soft triumph on a sunlit shore,
Or plunges in the darkness of the grave.

A LUTANIST.

O WELL-BELOVÈD lute,
Whence sweetest sounds have birth,
From thee I pluck the fruit
Of all my joy on earth.
I wear my queen's device,
And her white hand have kissed—
I dwell in Paradise,
I am her lutanist.

What have I more to seek?
Of old, erect and proud,
I went, with flushing cheek,
Through plaudits of the crowd.
I longed to soar on high,
Until one day I wist
That kings were less than I,
Who am her lutanist.

High in her stately house
My southern window shines,
All grown about with boughs
Of leafy, tangled vines.
My sovereignty is there,
A world of sky and song,
And little do I care
To gaze upon the throng.
The busy world below
May hurry on apace,
But by my heart I know
When, homeward from the chase,
My lady passes by,
Her falcon on her wrist—
Then from his turret high
Looks forth her lutanist.

I turn from watchful eyes,
Yet though I dream apart,
The drowsy music lies
Asleep within my heart,
Until she gives command—
Then at her voice it stirs,
And pours through heart and hand,
Which, being mine, are hers.
And thoughts that thrill and yearn,

And visions sought in vain,
Throng all around, and turn
To music in my brain.
A spell is in the air
That nothing may resist,
As I stand playing there
Who am her lutanist.

And stories have been told
Of me as half divine,
Till princes offer gold
To hear this skill of mine.
Yet I should linger mute
If my fair dame I missed—
For I am but the lute,
And she the lutanist !

A GAME OF PIQUET.

SEE, as you turn a page
Of Holbein's Dance of Death,
Across the narrow stage,
Drawing a hurried breath,
The sons of men go by,
Like a bewildered dream,
Beneath a changeless sky
An ever-changing stream.
Swiftly as driven clouds
They pass in love and strife,
And all the shifting crowds
Are busy with their life,
Eager, intent, and much
                    Perplexed.
Then comes the deadly touch—
                    What next?

We do not paint Death now,
As did those men of old,
(And, truly, I allow
They make my blood run cold,)
Yet the old fancy lives
In spite of growth and change,
And to our sorrow gives
Its humour grim and strange.
The bitter wine that when
We meet our mocking chance
Is stamped from souls of men
In Death's fantastic dance.
As when the cry of Love,
                    Or Hate,
Rings to the heaven above
                    Too late.

We need not paint the scene,
The skull, the grasping hand,
For that which once has been
Our hearts will understand.
A flower may be the sign
That calls your vision back,
Or just a pencil line
In some old almanac.

A pack of cards for me,
Where smiling queen and knave
Can bid me turn and see
A shadow and a grave,
Nor to my dying day
        Forget
How once I used to play
        Piquet.

Once, in a quaint old place !
My dreamy thoughts recall
Its somewhat faded grace
Of painting on the wall,
Pink roses ribbon-tied.
And pairs of snowy doves
Tall vases side by side,
And lightly flying Loves,
Such as our poets sing,
Or sang, some time ago,
Dan Cupid on the wing
With quiver, shafts, and bow—
But Love had there no need
        Of darts,
He simply gave the lead
        In Hearts.

Into the sunlit room
To break the half-played game,
With heavy stroke of doom,
The grief of parting came.
Strong in my happy love
I faced the bitter pain,
And swore by heaven above
We two would meet again.
Silent I saw her stand,
Pallid, in trouble sore,
While from her hanging hand
Slipped downward to the floor
Black cards, whose ominous
           Array
Fate had not suffered us
              To play.

I bade a brave farewell
Without a thought of fear,
Ah God !   I could not tell
That evil day was near,
When Life's glad music sank
To sobs, and died away,
When Earth's high mountains shrank
To one low heap of clay.
When I, aghast and sad,

Stood silent and apart,
When all Creation had
A sepulchre for heart.
No love the unknown land
       Invades,
And Death played out the hand
       Of Spades.

FIRST OR LAST?

A WIFE TO HER HUSBAND.

'My life ebbs from me—I must die,
Must die—it has a ghostly sound,
A far-off thunder drawing nigh
An echo as from underground.
Yes, I must die who fain would live;
You cannot give me life—alas !
Dear Love of mine, you can but give
One latest kiss before I pass.

Dear, we have had our summer bliss,
Kisses on cheek, and lip, and brow,
But soul to soul, as now we kiss,
I think we never kissed till now.
Give both your hands, and let the earth
Roll onward—let what will befall.
This is an hour of wondrous birth,
And can it be the end of all?

Ah, your sad face !　I know you think
(Clasp me, O love, your faith is mine,
Only my weakness made me shrink)
That I am standing on the brink
Of night where never dawn will shine,
Of slumber whence I shall not wake,
Of darkness where no life will grope—
I know your hopeless creed, and take
My part therein for your dear sake,—
We stand asunder if I hope.

. And yet I dreamed of a fair land
Where you and I were met at last,
And face to face, and hand in hand,
Smiled at the sorrow overpast.
The eastern sky was touched with fire,
In the dim woodlands cooed the dove,
Earth waited, tense with strong desire,
For day—your coming, O my love !
The breeze awoke to breathe your name,
And through the leafy maze I came,
With feet that could not turn aside,
With eyes that would not be denied—
My lips, my heart a rosy flame,
Because you kissed me ere I died.

Death could but part us for a while,
Beyond the boundary of years
We met again—O do not smile
That tender smile, more sad than tears !

Forget my vision sweet and vain,
Your faith is mine—your faith is best,
Let others count the joys they gain,
I am a thousand times more blest.
They can but give a scanty dole
Out of a life made safe in heaven,
While I am sovereign o'er the whole,
I can give all—and all is given !
Faith such as ours defies the grave,
Nor needs a dream of bliss above—
Shall not this moment make me brave?
O aloe-flower of perfect love !
What though the end of all be come,
The latest hour, the latest breath,
This is life's triumph, and its sum,
The aloe-flower of love and death !

And yet your kisses wake a life
That throbs in anguish through my heart,
Leaps up to wage despairing strife,
And shudders, loathing to depart.

Can such desire be born in vain—
Crushed by inevitable doom?
While you let live can Love be slain?
Can Love lie dead within my tomb?
And when you die—that hopeless day
When darkness comes and utmost need,
And I am dead and cold, you say,
Will Death have power to hold his prey?
Shall I not know? Shall I not heed?
When your last sun, with waning light,
Below the sad horizon dips,
Shall I not rush from out the night
To die once more upon your lips?

Ah, the black moment comes! Draw nigh,
Stoop down, O Love, and hold me fast.
O empty earth! O empty sky!
There is no answer, though I die
Breathing my soul out in the cry,
Is it the first kiss—or the last?'

A DREAM OF LIFE AND DEATH.

It was the golden time of ripened grain,
And in the drowsy sunlight slept a plain
Peaceful and fair.   The idly sighing breeze
Wandered through groves of summer-mellowed trees,
But in the centre was a guarded course
For runners, and the lists for feats of force ;
And these were ringed with multitudes of eyes,
And all the air was thrilled with long-drawn sighs,
While high above the ardour of the race
Sat Death, enthroned o'er all with quiet face.

I thought I gazed on him, and men drew near
Prepared for battle, saying, 'Have no fear.
True that he sits for ever throned on high,
And rules o'er all things, yet you shall not die.
True that, however strong, however fleet,
No man escapes the death that he must meet,
Yet face him boldly in the final strife,
Death is an empty name, and he is Life.'

And I believed.   But, waiting for that hour,
My eyes were drawn by a constraining power,
And fastened on the never-wavering eyes
Of the strange masquer, throned in kingly guise.
Where was the faintest change that should proclaim
Death as not wholly death ?   It never came.
His was a stillness earth has never known,
Not the white lifelessness of carven stone,
But perfect silence since the world began,
A pause, outlasting all the life of man.
God !   Did that haunting gaze see all, or nought ?
Were those eyes blank, or filled with awful thought ?

I gazed until the clamour of the place
Died utterly, and left me face to face
With Death, in strangest loneliness apart.
The pulses of my wildly throbbing heart
Beat time for all creation—I was life,
And he was Death—I waited for the strife.
When should it be ?   My soul within me burned,
And I poured forth the lesson I had learned.

' Hearken, O Death !   What cause have I for fear
Am not I armed to battle with thee here ?
Nameless am I, and thou of great renown,
Thou shalt o'erthrow me, thou shalt cast me down,

Yet by thy very touch I shall arise,
And thou in smiting shalt release thy prize.
Thou canst not conquer me, thou canst not give
A death-wound to the soul, foredoomed to live !'

Rising to wild defiance of my fears
My voice rang out, and echoed in my ears.
Far off, in warring waves I heard it roll
And die beneath the brooding calm.   My soul
With that intense and momentary strain,
Lifted the silence, but it sank again.

Slowly it sank upon the burdened air,
And flying Time—nought else was moving there—
Sped with hushed lips, nor spake of hours and days,
Beneath the great endurance of that gaze.
I waited, till a voice within me said,
'What shall Death do for thee, if Death be dead ?'

If Death be dead !   The sun, the arch of sky,
The air about me, seemed to reel and die.
Vain were the hopeful words of long ago,
And warlike armour was an empty show,
Hiding a traitor heart.   In cold despair,
Having no spirit more to do and dare,
I loosed the bands, and threw it all aside.
Then through my veins there rushed a quickening tide

Of life, delivered from an icy weight ;
And I once more could look upon my fate,
Once more I stood—I cried with hurrying breath,

' See, I will take thee now for very Death,
The end of all things, utter and complete,
And I, like them, shall lie beneath thy feet,
As nothing, in thy gulf of nothingness.
Yet I stand up before thee, none the less,
Not hoping to escape, since thou art sure,
But saying, While my lifetime may endure,
In joy, and pain, and wonder ; it is mine—
Only the blankness and the end are thine !
Is my life short ?   I measure not its flight,
Let me maintain it on a level height,
That I may look thee boldly in the eyes,
Not gazing upward as a suppliant dies.
Let me live nobly, nobly yield thee all—
Thou shalt preserve me, Death, from future fall ! '

I paused.   The summer breezes, lingering, sighed ;
There was no other, answer.   Then I cried,

' Nay, even if all mankind shall seem to me
Aimless, confused, an ever-weltering sea,
Breaking in ebb and flow against thy steep ;
And I myself a ripple on that deep,

Yet will I scorn thee—scorn all craven fears,
Flinging on high my handful of salt tears
To flash in lucid sunlight as I die—
And Death, if it be Death, will I defy !'
So spoke I while my heart-throbs came apace,

But still Death sits there, with the quiet face.

A STUDENT.

FOR him the past has poured her drowsy wine;
   And, turning from all beauty 'neath the sun,
Ever he seeks the dim horizon line,
   Regions afar, where earth and sky are one.
Here, in this central moment of to-day,
High heaven seems so very far away.

Sadness there is, not sorrow, on his brow,
   He shrinks alike from laughter and from tears,
When happier glances hail the budding bough,
   He tracks the footsteps of departed years,
Where, faintly dim, their memories linger yet
All grown about with moss and violet.

His fellow men our student little heeds;
   His pathway lies 'mid visionary throngs—
Spring, though he meets her in the daisied meads,
   Lives for him only in her ancient songs;
Nay, very Love himself he does but know
A boy, with bow and arrows, long ago.

He cannot feel for human hopes and fears,
 All hopes and fears are chronicled for him,
Unnoticed glides his little span of years,
 His eyes are fixed on ages vast and dim.
He dreams of bygone days, with thoughtful brow,
Till Life stands still, and, startled, whispers 'Now!'

PRIVATE THEATRICALS.[1]

BEFORE THE CURTAIN RISES.

THE guests assemble.   Down the stairs I steal,
  As if I'd dressed a century before,
And pause, a courtly beau from head to heel,
  Close by the green-room door.

The fire-light glows within ; the leaping blaze
  Shines on an eager face.   What happy spell
Summoned that sweetest glimpse of olden days,
  That arch and radiant belle ?

Ready to play her part in quaint disguise
  Of powdered hair and old brocaded gown,
She warms a dainty foot, nor turns her eyes
  Where, with an anxious frown,

---

[1] First published in the *Century* for September 1884.

Conning his book, our crafty Villain sits ;
   Tall, handsome, honest, he's a wealthy squire—
A trifle heavy—in our telling bits
   He rather misses fire.

I push the door, and meet a smile from each :
   My lady's eyes are lifted from the flame ;
.The Villain keeps his finger on a speech,
   And greets me by my name.

I am the happy hero of the play,
   With Love, and Luck, and Valour on my side ;
I am to conquer everything to-day,
   I am to win my bride.

And I will win her !   Ah, they do not know—
   Well may they praise me as I act my part !
This courtship of a hundred years ago
   Is living in my heart.

Yet I can plead my cause without the aid
   Of studied phrases—they are poor and weak ;
Wait only till our comedy is played—
   This is no time to speak.

The actors hurry in, and one and all
   Appeal to me to listen or to look.
The footman's livery is a size too small,
   The prompter wants his book.

My father comes to show his wrinkled face,
   And loiters nervously behind the scenes ;
I praise his baldness and his feeble pace,—
   He's only in his teens !

There are so many duties to perform,
   And at a moment's notice I must say
Who is to see about the thunder-storm,
   And who takes in the tray.

Where is the fatal deed that must be signed ?
   I give them all their answers, and by chance,
Lounging beside the window, lift the blind
   And cast a careless glance.

Nothing to see—how heavily it rains !—
   Nothing but here and there a gliding spark,
Where carriages along the country lanes
   Come rolling through the dark.

Beyond, there lies a world of gloom unknown ;
　　Our little space of glitter, warmth, and light
Is but a many-coloured bubble, blown
　　On a black sea of night.

Well, let the bubble break without a sigh,
　　And let to-morrow come, as come it will ;
I am the happy hero till I die,
　　If she is with me still !

And when hereafter we recall this day
　　Of painted, powdered courtship from the past,
We'll laugh at stage and prompter, while I play
　　The lover to the last !

AFTER THE CURTAIN FALLS.

All's over now.　It was a great success.
　　Our honest Villain did the best he could ;
Took pains, and plodded through his wickedness,--
　　He's really very good ;

And when he drove the lady to despair
　　With darkly scowling threats and feigned alarms,
I rushed upon the stage, defied him there,
　　And clasped her in my arms !

An explanation followed.   I embraced
  A few relations, quite unknown till then ;
Virtue was lucky, Villainy disgraced—
  We all were better men.

Then came my wrinkled sire—'Nay, I mistook—
  You won't bear malice for a blunder—zounds !
Take your old father's gift—a pocket-book,'—
  'Twas twenty thousand pounds.

'Bless you, my children !   She's a pearl, my boy !'
  The others gathered round for their farewell,
And stood in attitudes, and wished us joy,
  And so the curtain fell.

They called us back.   The laughing plaudits swelled
  To welcome us.   That moment was divine—
The token of my triumph !   As I held
  My darling's hand in mine,

I seemed to feel her happy pulses beat,
  As mine were beating in my joy and pride ;
I trod the whole world underneath my feet
  Since she was by my side !

And then—why, as we passed, I overheard
   A hurried whisper, caught a meaning smile :
Enough—it was the Villain she preferred—
   The Villain all the while !

That was the end, and here I am alone,
   Dismally laughing at my sorry plight ;
I listen to the wind's unceasing moan,
   I gaze into the night,

Only to see my pale reflection cast
   Upon the gloom.   A bitter lash of rain
Falls, with a sudden fury of the blast,
   On the black window-pane.

She loves him—loves him !   She will be his wife !
   And strangely I recall, as here I stand,
How in another world, another life,
   I bowed, and dropped her hand.

What did I think of as I bent my head ?
   The fire-light flashed upon my buckled shoes—
Poor hero !   Well, there's nothing to be said—
   Was she not free to choose ?

She did not know !   With my whole heart I played.
   What then ?   She thought I acted well, no doubt ;
If Love came stealing through the masquerade,
   How should she find him out ?

She did not know !   God bless her in her choice !
   (Ay, and the Villain too!)   No thought of blame
Shall ever lend its hardness to my voice,
   When I would speak her name.

There will be other plays in coming years
   When this is half forgotten ; there will be
New scenes, new dresses, and new hopes and fears—
   But this old play for me !

One can't be always learning things by heart ;
   Variety is charming—yet it palls.
' Zounds ! '—(as the father said)—I'll play my part
   Until the curtain falls !

OF THE PAST.[1]

WHITE flowers lie upon her breast :
Her throbbing pulses are at rest ;
A circlet glimmers on her head ;
She is a queen, and she is dead.

Around her all is very still ;
Unchanged, behind a changeless hill,
The western sun for ever dips,
And dying splendours kiss her lips.

Her passive hand a sceptre holds ;
Her raiment falls in stately folds ;
Her lashes slumber on her cheek :
The world would listen did she speak.

[1] First published in *Harper's Magazine* for February 1884.

She will be still for evermore :
Though crownèd king or emperor
Made bare his treasury for her,
The quiet lips will never stir.

She will be still ; but all around,
Voices, which speak without a sound,
Bid tender chords awake and thrill,
Telling of her, though she is still—

Telling how days had wingèd feet,
How childish nights had slumber sweet,
And little many-coloured dreams
Shone through the dark in fitful gleams

Then kindly Nature round us curled,
The skies bent down to clasp the world,
And every star, a beacon-light,
Was steadfast on its stately height.

Content, we fronted wonders new,
Rainbow and thunder, fire and dew,
And deemed the very highway sod
Untrodden till we came and trod.

I

And golden were the days of youth,
When all was beauty, joy, and truth,
When sordid wealth was nothing worth,
For Love in splendour walked the earth.

O sweet untroubled vision, stay !
Cease, thou importunate To-day,
Cease eager toil, and clamour shrill !
We are with her—and she is still.

A TOWN GARDEN.[1]

A PLOT of ground—the merest scrap—
  Deep, like a dry, forgotten well,
A garden caught in a brick-built trap,
  Where men make money, buy and sell ;
And struggling through the stagnant haze,
  Dim flowers, with sapless leaf and stem,
Look up with something of the gaze
  That homesick eyes have cast on them.

There is a rose against the wall,
  With scanty, smoke-incrusted leaves ;
Fair showers on happier roses fall—
  On this, foul droppings from the eaves.
It pines, but you need hardly note ;
  It dies by inches in the gloom ;
Shoots in the spring-time, as if by rote ;
  Long has forgotten to dream of bloom.

[1] First published in *Harper's Magazine* for August 1883.

The poorest blossom, and it were classed
   With colour and name—but never a flower !
It blooms with the roses whose bloom is past,
   Of every hue, and place, and hour.
They live before me as I look—
   The damask buds that breathe and glow,
Pink wild roses, down by a brook,
   Lavish clusters of airy snow.

Could one transplant you—(far on high
   A murky sunset lights the tiles)—
And set you 'neath the arching sky,
   In the green country, many miles,
Would you strike deep and suck up strength,
   Washed with rain and hung with pearls,
Cling to the trellis, a leafy length,
   Sweet with blossom for June and girls ?

Yet no ! Who needs you in those bowers ?
   Who prizes gifts that all can give ?
Bestow your life instead of flowers,
   And slowly die that dreams may live.
Prisoned and perishing, your dole
   Of lingering leaves shall not be vain—
Worthy to wreathe the hemlock bowl,
   Or twine about the cross of pain !

ALMOND BLOSSOM.[1]

LOVE, will you yet regret the flowers that lie
Scattered, and wet with tears from April's sky?
They are not dead—the flowers can never die.

They are the gladness of a world unworn;
They sleep and waken with it, night and morn,
And laugh our dreams of ancient days to scorn.

O'er the wide gulfs that part us from the past,
O'er ruins of great works designed to last,
The lightly woven chain of flowers is cast;

And odours of old gardens, faintly blown
From legendary days and shores unknown,
Blend with the breath of those our hands have sown.

[1] First published in *Harper's Magazine* for August 1881.

Of Milton's world how much was doomed to pass
And yet we linger on the daisied grass,
And pluck the flowers he plucked for Lycidas,

And still the spring-time crowns a waiting land
With tender bloom.   Nay, Love, 'tis you who stand
With almond clusters in your clasping hand,

And all the sunset heaven behind your head ;
'Tis you must pass, an unknown way to tread,
And leave the flowers.   If I had long been dead,

Yet came from sleep of twilight centuries,
The almond blossom 'neath these vernal skies
Should welcome me again, but not your eyes.

The rosy petals, drifted on the breeze,
Might strew, as now, the turf beneath the trees.
As now ? No, not as now.   Because to these

Pink sprays of almond, for a little space
Your musing smile, your blossom-perfect face,
Give a supreme and solitary grace.

OCTOBER.[1]

Long looked for was the summer.   Anxious eyes
   Noted the budding bough, the crocus flame,
That told its coming.   Now, 'neath autumn skies
   The leaves fall slowly, slowly as they came.

There is no need to watch while winter weaves
   Fair buds to crown another golden prime,
For something heavier than the autumn leaves
   Has hidden eyes that looked for summer-time.

The trees shall wake from their forgetful sleep
   Unto new blossom and a tender green—
The countless trees !—but never one will keep
   A little leaf or flower that she has seen !

[1] First published in *Harper's Magazine* for November 1880.

FROM 'MITCHELHURST PLACE.'

AT HER PIANO.

'IT chanced I loitered through a room,
Dusk with a shaded, sultry gloom,
And full of memories of old times—
I lingered, shaping into rhymes
My visions of those earlier days
'Mid their neglected waifs and strays ;
A yellowing keyboard caught my gaze,
And straight I fancied, as I stood
Resting my hand on polished wood,
Letting my eyes contented trace
The daintiness of inlaid grace,
That Music's ghost, outworn and spent,
Dreamed near her antique instrument.

'But when I broke its silence, fain
To call an echo back again
Of some old-fashioned, tender strain,

Played once by player long since dead—
I found my dream of music fled !
The chords I wakened could but speak
In jangled utterance, thin and weak,
In shallow discords, as when age
Reaches its last decrepit stage,
In feeble notes that seemed to chide—
This was the end ! I stepped aside,
In my impatient weariness,
Into the window's draped recess ;
Without, was all the joy of June,
Within, a piano out of tune !

' But while, half-hidden, thus I stayed,
There came in one who lightly laid
White hands upon the yellow keys
To seek their lingering harmonies.
I think she sighed—I know she smiled—
And straightway Music was beguiled,
And all the faded by-gone years,
With all their by-gone hopes and fears,
Their long-forgotten smiles and tears,
Their empty dreams that meant sq much,
Began to sing beneath her touch.

' The notes that Time had taught to fret,
Racked with a querulous regret,

Forsook their burden of complaint
For melodies more sweetly faint
Than lovers ever dreamed in sleep—
Than rippling murmurs of the deep—
Than whispered hope of endless peace
Ah, let her play or let her cease,
For still that sound is in the air,
And still I see her seated there !

  'Yet, even as her fingers ranged,
I knew those jangled notes unchanged ;
My soul had heard, in ear's despite,
And Love had made the music right.'

AUTUMN BERRIES.

'Speech was forbidden me ; I could but stay,
Ambushed behind a leafless hawthorn screen,
And look upon her passing.   She had been
To pluck red berries on that autumn day,
And Love, who from her side will never stray,
Stole some for pity, seeing me unseen,
And sighing, let them fall, that I might glean—
'Poor gift,' quoth he, 'that Time shall take away !'

Nay but I mock at Time ! It shall not be
That, fleet of foot, he robs me of my prize ;
Her smile has kindled all the sullen skies,
Blessed the dull furrows and the leafless tree,
And year by year the autumn, ere it dies,
Shall bring my rosy treasure back to me ! '

SONNET.

' Have not all songs been sung—all loves been told ?
What shall I say when nought is left unsaid ?
The world is full of memories of the dead—
Echoes and relics.   Here's no virgin gold,
But all assayed, none left for me to mould
Into new coin, and at your feet to shed ;
Each piece is mint-marked with some poet's head,
Tested and rung in tributes manifold.

' Oh for a single word should be mine own,
And not the homage of long-studied art,
Common to all, for you who stand apart !
Oh weariness of measures tried and known !
Yet in their rhythm, you—if you alone—
Should hear the passionate pulses of my heart ! '

A WISH

IF I could find the Little Year,
The Happy Year, the glad New Year—
If I could find him setting forth
To seek the ancient track—
I'd bring him here, the Little Year,
Like a pedlar with his pack.

And all of golden brightness,
And nothing dull or black,
And all that heart could fancy,
And all that heart could lack,
Should be your share of the pedlar's ware,
When he undid his pack.

The best from out his treasure
A smile of yours would coax,
And then we'd speed him on his way,
At midnight's failing strokes ;
And bid him hurry round the world,
And serve the other folks !

MOTHER AND CHILD.[1]

BITTER blasts and vapours dim —
What had they to do with him?
Spring, though she was far away,
Took dominion for a day,
Filled the air with breathings soft,
Bade a skylark sing aloft,
When we laid him in his bed,
Cloudless blue above his head.

It was not for him to reach
Manly height, and thought, and speech,
Not to climb untrodden steeps,
Not to search out unknown deeps,
Not through warring joy and pain
Kingliness of soul to gain.

[1] First published in the *Century* for April 1883.

He had only baby words,
Little music, like the birds,
Sweetly inarticulate,
Nothing wise, nor high, nor great.
Sunny smiles and kisses sweet—
White and softly childish feet—
Curls that floated on the breeze—
We remember him for these.

They are weary who are wise.
He looked up with happy eyes,
Little knowing, little seeing,
Only praising God by being.

Oh, the life we could not save !
Do not say, above his grave,
That the fair and darling face
Was but lent a little space
Till the Father called him back,
By an unknown homeward track.
No, though Death came darkly chill—
Bade the beating heart be still,
Touching him with fingers cold—
What was given still we hold ;
Though he died, as die the flowers,
He for evermore is ours.

Ours, though we must travel soon
Onward through Life's afternoon ;
Shadows, falling long and grey,
Gather round the western day,
And our twilight visions show
How the years shall come and go.

Little maids, with tangled curls,
Change to slender, dreamy girls ;
Chubby rogues grow tall, and then
Go their way as bearded men.
And the mother stands aside,
With an ache beneath her pride,
And a sorrow 'mid her joys,
For the vanished babes and boys ;
So the earlier gladness wanes—
But the little one remains.

For a house that once has known
Tiny feet on stair and stone—
Steps that never more shall sound,
Feet at rest beneath the ground—
Keeps remembrance of the dead,
And the music of their tread.
Not at noonday, busy, bright,
Only in the quiet night,

With a thrill of sweetest pain,
Comes that music once again,
Heard in stillness and apart
Echoed from his mother's heart.

MICHAELMAS DAISIES.[1]

DAISIES on the emerald lawn,
Daisies rosy-white for dawn,
  Rosy-white for summer's dawn,
Michaelmas daisies grey and drear,
Dusk for the dusky close of the year,
  Michaelmas daisies for close of the year.

The year is old, and the weary wind
  Withers its glory, leaf by leaf,
Gone is the garland that April twined,
  Gone, June roses, and August sheaf.
The apples are gone from the orchard boughs,
  Faded the creeper's tangled grace,
The bitter blast from its rest must rouse,
  For winter comes on, apace, apace,

[1] First published in the *Spectator*, April 1870.

K

The old year dreams of its daisied dawn,
  All gölden-bright, and rosy-white,
Dreams of its daisies like stars on the lawn,
  And makes them again in the dusk of the night.

Daisies on the emerald lawn,
Daisies rosy-white for dawn,
  Rosy-white for summer's dawn,
Michaelmas daisies grey and drear,
Dusk for the dusky close of the year,
  Michaelmas daisies for close of the year.

A CLOSED BOOK.

I READ it long ago, and as I read,
 A world of wonder rose before my eyes
And widened into vastness, dimly spread
    'Neath solemn skies.

Beyond the page my emulous desire
 Divined the marvels of unwritten scenes,—
I was ambitious, by the school-room fire,
    Just in my teens !

Now, though the book has faded out of mind,
 Though all that dreamy pageant I forget,
Its shadow lingers, vast and undefined,
    And haunts me yet.

The far-off glory dies in pallid gleams,—
 Cannot a yearning sigh the flame restore ?
Cannot I read again, and dream those dreams
    Once more,—once more ?

¹ First published in the *Spectator* of January 13, 1877.

Never.   The child has passed away, the book
  Is closed, and 'mid my childish memories laid,
With all its magic in it.   I would look,
             But am afraid.

Men do not name it 'mid immortal works,
  And laggard Fame is slow to find it out.
Perhaps.   And yet within my soul there lurks
             Something of doubt.

How if the visions whose dim figures thickened
  Round me, and thronged my yet unpeopled air,—
How if the fear, whereat my pulses quickened,
             Should not be there?

How if the shadow, awful in its gloom,
  Were dwarfed and shrivelled when the daylight
    dawned,—
How if I smiled above the empty tomb,—
             How if I yawned?

How if I marvelled to myself, and him
  I honoured once?   Surely the Past might rise
In human shape, and look at me with dim
             Reproachful eyes,

Because for his enchantment long ago
   I had no thanks to give in later days,—-
O dreams that flickered in the firelight glow,
            Be his your praise !

He gave my fancy wings, and in its flight,
   No fault, no failure, could it stoop to note ;
Perhaps I read the book he meant to write,
            Not that he wrote.

Why should the knowledge that in awe began
   Be ended now in laughter barbed with pain ?
And why take back the faith that never can
            Be given again ?

No, he shall keep it ! Do not draw the curtain,
   Let my dim wonder be a wonder still,—
I will not read it,—I am almost certain
            I never will !

A BIRTHDAY WISH.

(L. A. I., MARCH 10, 1881.)

'TIME flies' they say.   Perhaps it's just as well
    To watch him flying and not wish to stay him,—
Especially as I don't know the spell
            That *could* delay him !

And if he paused 'twould trouble folks who take
    A yearly due of rent, and rate and tax,
And might confuse the thoughtful souls who make
            Our almanacks.

No, let him fly !   But as he hurries on
    Would he but hear my birthday wish !   He should
Take nought away of happiness bygone,
            Bring nought but good.

He should not point to memories half effaced,
   Nor dole the sands of life in scanty measure,
Time, like an eager messenger, should haste
            To do your pleasure.

He should bring hope to gladden all the year,
   Hope with no lingering shadow of regret,
And, passing, make the home that you hold dear
            Still dearer yet.

He should not change the friends who round you stand,
   But added names upon his record trace,
The circle should not know a loosened hand,
            A missing face.

No thought of sadness should his passing leave,
   No ! evermore so lightly should he fly
That only by his gifts could you perceive
            Time had gone by.

Ah ! but enough of this !   I fear lest you
   Should laugh at foolish thought and clumsy rhyme.
Foolish ?   Perhaps.   But that's what *I* would do
            If I were Time !

A CHRISTMAS CARD.

To J. P. S.

Ere yet, Old Year, sore wounded with my pain,
You go from out the Present to the Past,
I charge you with an errand for the last.

Tell her my Christmas thoughts are hers again,
Tell her, O year, I long that she may live
Glad in all gifts that all good years can give.

And if hereafter there must come an hour
Heavy with loss and lengthened out in sorrow,
Black with the night, and threatened by the morrow,

Tell her I hope that even *that* may flower
With loving thought—may bloom for her no less
Than mine for me with her sweet tenderness !

A CHRISTMAS CARD.

SWEET SISTER mine, I fain would have you look
Backward on life, as 'twere a painted book,
And turn the written leaves until they show
Records of Christmas Gladness long ago.
Of Christmas holidays and Christmas toys—·
The waits—the bells that woke us to our joys—
Then turn beyond those pictures bright and small
To the vague colours that precede them all.
Yet shall you never find the whole book through,
One Christmas earlier than my love for you.

138

A CHRISTMAS CARD.

To E. I.

1879--1885.

It was the heart of summer when
　I knew your smile and greeting first,
And though the years have fled since then,
　With seasons o'er and o'er rehearsed,

The sunlight of that day remains.
　'Tis with me now, through fog and rime
And winter's hail, and autumn's rains
　Hold something of that summer-time.

So let December scowl and weep!
　May you in charmèd brightness live,
And ever, ever, may you keep
　The sunny gladness that you give!

A CHRISTMAS CARD.

To E. I.

'Fair thoughts and happy hours attend you.'—SHAKESPEARE.

I BUY my card, and find thereon
    Great *Shakespeare's* self good-will expressing !
And that prolific scribe ' *Anon.*'
    The best of hopes to you addressing ;

I yield possession, scarcely loth,
    Since I can slip a line between,
To tell you I defy them both
    To *say* ought sweeter than I *mean !*

' May Christmas come laden with every blessing ! '

December 1884.

HIS CALENDAR.[1]

(STEENIE.)

KINDLY Fates ! I pray you hear !
   May a small but happy star,
Shining through the joyous year,
   Rule his little calendar !

May his days be marked with white—
   White of newly-fallen snow,
White of orchards, for delight
   Of the coloured fruit shall grow.

May his days be rose and green,
   With the blossom and the leaf—
Golden-bright with sunny sheen,
   Never, never grey with grief.

May his days be brightly blue,
   Where the ocean salt is wide,
Ever old and ever new,
   Hurries in with crested tide.

[1] First published in the ' Bairn's Annual,' 1887.

Sweet be they with song of birds,
  Sweet with sound of falling streams,
Sweet beyond all spoken words,
  Beautiful with childish dreams.

Hence ! all shapes of angry strife,
  Evil Fortune, stand afar !
Never cloud his sunny life,
  Never blot his calendar !

ONE OF THE MULTITUDE.

WHEN I am dead !
  When all my world of thought
  Has crumbled into nought,
When my last word is said,
When I have laid me down upon my bed,
  And shut my eyes on love and strife,
      On woven joys and pains—
  When the vast tide of onward-rushing life
Has ebbed for ever from my shrunken veins—
O God ! how will it be when I am dead ?

  Above my head
  The April grass will grow,
  The starry daisies blow,
  All things will come again,
  Blossom, and ripened grain,

The sun will shine, the wayward wind will roam
　And softly fall the rain
　　While I lie low
Beneath the far-off blue of the unchanging dome.

If those who hold me dear,
　Who loved, and love me yet,
In tender memory, and mournful fear,
　A stone above my burial-place shall set,
　To tell my name in days when all forget,
　　Bright Nature shall draw near
　　　And, smiling, spoil
The record, cut with melancholy toil.

Her softly busy fingers will efface
　The token of their care.
　With sun, and summer showers,
　With growth of moss and flowers,
With lichen creeping stealthily apace,
　Will she, through many a gliding day and week,
Unwearied—O most pitiless and fair !—
　Destroy the letters dim, the latest words I speak,
　　Till nought remains to tell
That ever I have lived, who loved her once so well !

When I am dead !—am dead !
And past all reach of hopes and fears,
   Before some loving eyes
   My face, perhaps, may rise
Seen dimly through a tender mist of tears.
My memory a little space will stand
Upon the borders of the living land ;
   Encircled with a quiet light
    Whose gentle rays
Are pale reflections from my sunlit days.
   A little while shall I remain,
Calm, with a calmness nothing can destroy,
   A shadow, 'mid the phantoms of my pain,
A shadow, 'mid the phantoms of my joy,
   And then the light must wane.

O bitter fate —alas !
Out of the lives I love my life must pass,
   Must slowly fade away.
They shall be sad—but all my tears are shed !
Shall triumph—all my words of praise are said—
Shall hope—I have no pressure of the hand—
Shall dream—I might not even understand
   When I am dead,
And newer visions come in old hopes' stead.

And if, when I am gone,
Some words of mine live on,
They shall be only, in the world's great day,
Like a brief echo that from far away
    Comes with familiar sound.
It wavers to and fro between the hills
        Above, around,
    The silent air it fills
With lonely speech that knows no change,
    But wanders, clear and strange,
And has no help of living lips or eyes.
A little while the sound may go and come
    Though he who uttered it be dumb,
A little while it lingers ere it dies.

    Thus shall it chance to me
    In ages yet to be,
There shall remain no trace on land or sea,
Nor in the memory of any friend,
But they and it shall surely have an end.

    Better it should be so,
    Better that all should go ;
I have been glad to breathe the summer air,
And I have lived, rejoicing in the sun,
But when my gladness in the world is done,

L

Shall I desire to leave my shadow there ?
Shall I repine that all my thought and care
   Must needs be hid
Within the narrow grave where I have made my bed ?
Why do I fear oblivion?　God forbid
That Nature should be conscious of the dead !

  Then should the clouds o'erhead,
  Weaving a sable pall,
  Hang gloomily and low,
  Burdened with hopeless woe.
  Then mournfully should fall
  The slowly dropping showers
  Upon the silent earth—
An earth that had no heart to deck herself with
  flowers.
  The wildly flowing streams
  Of song birds rippling mirth,
Should die in lamentations, or should grow
To sad complaining, as in restless dreams.
  Across the misty height—
  In brief and melancholy gleams
  Where the dark veil was torn—
The ghastly sun should hurry, pale and shorn,
To hide his aching eyes within the gloom
  And blackness of his tomb.

So should he yield his empire to the Night,
   And stars should burn on high,
Sad funeral tapers in the hollow sky.
The weary wind should wander and complain,
   Seeking the dead, in vain,
   Yearning in helpless pain.
The withered reeds should whisper by the meres;
The dry leaves cling to every summer tree,
   Recalling bygone years ;
And all the heavy waters of the sea
   Should be most bitter tears.

   Not so ! For Nature lives
Untroubled—with full hands her bounty gives,
Nor heeds the generations she has nursed.
   But, while we come and go
   Like tides that ebb and flow,
Wears, though her children die, the smile she wore at
   first.

Our fellow-men forget us. Should we ask
   In their remembrance to remain,
   An aching sense of loss and pain,
An added burden in their daily task,
   A yearning, sad as vain?
O God forbid ! When the mysterious veil

Shall fall behind us, not to rise again,
Let memory grow pure, and sweet, and pale,
    Then let it fail.

For even now too many tears are wept,
Too many sighs make sad the summer's breath,
Too many buds enfold a gnawing death,
    Throughout this world of ours.
Too many nights pass, and we have not slept,
Too many days have heavy-footed hours ;
    Therefore do I accept,
    Well satisfied at heart,
Oblivion, which shall one day be my part.

    But there are summers past,
    Dim years of long ago,
Lost in the shadow that the ages cast
    Of which we nothing know,
    Since in the world of men
    Live none, were living then,
And none have made a record of those days,
But silently they sped, with all their blame and praise.

    Yet may we say, although
        We nothing know,
That those dim summers, vanished long ago,

Had silver twilight hours—
All the broad splendour of the noonday glow—
The joy of flowers.
That they had hyacinth and eglantine,
June roses, with their perfect petals curled
Over a heart of sweetness, dewy pearled ;
And lilies tall and white, and purple-clustered vine.
O blossoms sweet and far,
Which were, and are not, yet for ever are !
Leaves which no eyes of ours have seen,
Which long ago were shed,
Forgotten, withered, dead,
Yet live for ever in undying green !
Is there no place for me ?
Would that my life might be,
In the great future that is drawing near,
Like a forgotten flower, in a forgotten year !